Islam

Opposing Viewpoints®

Other Books of Related Interest

Islam

Opposing Viewpoints®

Jennifer A. Hurley, *Book Editor*

David L. Bender, *Publisher*
Bruno Leone, *Executive Editor*
Bonnie Szumski, *Editorial Director*
Stuart B. Miller, *Managing Editor*

OPPOSING VIEWPOINTS® SERIES

Greenhaven Press, Inc., San Diego, California

Library of Congress Cataloging-in-Publication Data

Islam : opposing viewpoints / Jennifer A. Hurley, editor.
      p.   cm. — (Opposing viewpoints series)
   Includes bibliographical references and index.
   ISBN 0-7377-0513-2 (pbk. : alk. paper) —
ISBN 0-7377-0514-0 (lib. bdg. : alk. paper)
   1. Islam—20th century. 2. Islamic fundamentalism.
3. Women in Islam. 4. Islamic countries—Relations—Europe.
5. Europe—Relations—Islamic countries. 6. United States—
Relations—Islamic countries. 7. Islamic countries—
Relations—United States. I. Hurley, Jennifer A., 1973–   .
II. Opposing viewpoints series (Unnumbered).

BP163 .I7327 2001
297.2'6—dc21   00-029359
                                                       CIP

Greenhaven Press, Inc., P.O. Box 289009
San Diego, CA 92198-9009

"Congress shall make
no law...abridging the
freedom of speech, or of
the press."

First Amendment to the U.S. Constitution

The basic foundation of our democracy is the First
Amendment guarantee of freedom of expression. The
Opposing Viewpoints Series is dedicated to the
concept of this basic freedom and the idea that it is
more important to practice it than to enshrine it.

Contents

Why Consider Opposing Viewpoints?

"The only way in which a human being can make some approach to knowing the whole of a subject is by hearing what can be said about it by persons of every variety of opinion and studying all modes in which it can be looked at by every character of mind. No wise man ever acquired his wisdom in any mode but this."

John Stuart Mill

In our media-intensive culture it is not difficult to find differing opinions. Thousands of newspapers and magazines and dozens of radio and television talk shows resound with differing points of view. The difficulty lies in deciding which opinion to agree with and which "experts" seem the most credible. The more inundated we become with differing opinions and claims, the more essential it is to hone critical reading and thinking skills to evaluate these ideas. Opposing Viewpoints books address this problem directly by presenting stimulating debates that can be used to enhance and teach these skills. The varied opinions contained in each book examine many different aspects of a single issue. While examining these conveniently edited opposing views, readers can develop critical thinking skills such as the ability to compare and contrast authors' credibility, facts, argumentation styles, use of persuasive techniques, and other stylistic tools. In short, the Opposing Viewpoints Series is an ideal way to attain the higher-level thinking and reading skills so essential in a culture of diverse and contradictory opinions.

In addition to providing a tool for critical thinking, Opposing Viewpoints books challenge readers to question their own strongly held opinions and assumptions. Most people form their opinions on the basis of upbringing, peer pressure, and personal, cultural, or professional bias. By reading carefully balanced opposing views, readers must directly confront new ideas as well as the opinions of those with whom they disagree. This is not to simplistically argue that everyone who reads opposing views will—or should—change his or her opinion. Instead, the series enhances readers' understanding of their own views by encouraging confrontation with opposing ideas. Careful examination of others' views can lead to the readers' understanding of the logical inconsistencies in their own opinions, perspective on why they hold an opinion, and the consideration of the possibility that their opinion requires further evaluation.

Evaluating Other Opinions

To ensure that this type of examination occurs, Opposing Viewpoints books present all types of opinions. Prominent spokespeople on different sides of each issue as well as well-known professionals from many disciplines challenge the reader. An additional goal of the series is to provide a forum for other, less known, or even unpopular viewpoints. The opinion of an ordinary person who has had to make the decision to cut off life support from a terminally ill relative, for example, may be just as valuable and provide just as much insight as a medical ethicist's professional opinion. The editors have two additional purposes in including these less known views. One, the editors encourage readers to respect others' opinions—even when not enhanced by professional credibility. It is only by reading or listening to and objectively evaluating others' ideas that one can determine whether they are worthy of consideration. Two, the inclusion of such viewpoints encourages the important critical thinking skill of objectively evaluating an author's credentials and bias. This evaluation will illuminate an author's reasons for taking a particular stance on an issue and will aid in readers' evaluation of the author's ideas.

As series editors of the Opposing Viewpoints Series, it is our hope that these books will give readers a deeper understanding of the issues debated and an appreciation of the complexity of even seemingly simple issues when good and honest people disagree. This awareness is particularly important in a democratic society such as ours in which people enter into public debate to determine the common good.

Those with whom one disagrees should not be regarded as enemies but rather as people whose views deserve careful examination and may shed light on one's own.

Thomas Jefferson once said that "difference of opinion leads to inquiry, and inquiry to truth." Jefferson, a broadly educated man, argued that "if a nation expects to be ignorant and free . . . it expects what never was and never will be." As individuals and as a nation, it is imperative that we consider the opinions of others and examine them with skill and discernment. The Opposing Viewpoints Series is intended to help readers achieve this goal.

David L. Bender & Bruno Leone,
Series Editors

Greenhaven Press anthologies primarily consist of previously published material taken from a variety of sources, including periodicals, books, scholarly journals, newspapers, government documents, and position papers from private and public organizations. These original sources are often edited for length and to ensure their accessibility for a young adult audience. The anthology editors also change the original titles of these works in order to clearly present the main thesis of each viewpoint and to explicitly indicate the opinion presented in the viewpoint. These alterations are made in consideration of both the reading and comprehension levels of a young adult audience. Every effort is made to ensure that Greenhaven Press accurately reflects the original intent of the authors included in this anthology.

Introduction

"Unnoticed by most Westerners, war has been unilaterally declared on Europe and the United States. Fundamentalists are responding to what they see as a centuries-long conspiracy by the West to destroy Islam."
> —Daniel Pipes, director of the Middle East Forum,
> National Interest, *Fall 1995*

"The Muslim world has been designated all too frequently as constituting a new 'other,' a rising, 'fundamentalist' challenge to everything that is best in Western and Christian civilization."
> —Antony T. Sullivan, associate at the Center
> for Middle Eastern and North African
> Studies, World & I, *September 1997*

According to the history of Islam, around the year 610 A.D., in a cave in the Arabian city of Mecca, a young orphan named Muhammad heard a voice ordering him to recite revelations that would be dictated to him. Over a period of 22 years, Muhammad acted as a "transmitter" for the words of God, or "Allah," which were recorded in writing and are collectively known as the Qur'an. Islam is based on the belief that the Qur'an is the direct word of God. Muslims, people who follow the Islamic faith, must observe the "five pillars" of Islam: the profession of faith in God and in the prophet Muhammad, prayer conducted five times a day, giving alms to the poor, fasting during the holy month of Ramadan, and undertaking the *hajj*, a pilgrimage to Mecca. In addition, the *Shari'ah*, Islam's legal-ethical system, provides Muslims with a blueprint for human conduct regarding matters such as family life and money.

The second-largest religion in existence (behind Christianity) and the dominant religion in more than twenty countries, Islam is believed to be practiced by over one-fifth of the world's population. As Islam's influence continues to grow throughout the Middle East, North Africa, and

12

in the West—where some say it is the fastest-growing religion— scholars of diverse nations and faiths have offered their perspectives about the impact of this development. One of the most controversial opinions has come from American professor Samuel P. Huntington, author of the 1996 book *The Clash of Civilizations and the Remaking of the World Order*. Huntington proposes that Islam and the West are embroiled in a "clash of civilizations" in which "dedicated Islamic militants exploit the open societies of the West and plant car bombs at selected targets [and] Western military professionals exploit the open skies of Islam and drop smart bombs at selected targets." In Huntington's view, this conflict between Islam and the West promises to end in violence.

Those who agree with Huntington maintain that the values of Islam and the West are inherently incompatible. For example, unlike Western societies, which tend toward secular governments, many societies in which Muslims are the majority support the integration of religion and government—a philosophy that is often referred to as "political Islam." Some Westerners regard political Islam as a dangerous movement whose goal is to gain power, dismantle other religions, and suppress human rights—as illustrated by Afghanistan, where self-proclaimed Islamic rulers have denied women basic rights such as access to health care; and Algeria and Sudan, where Christians have suffered persecution. Daniel Pipes, director of the Middle East Forum, contends that political Islam is by nature undemocratic and power-seeking:

> To build a new Muslim society, fundamentalists proclaim their intent to do whatever they must; they openly flaunt an extremist sensibility. . . . If that means destruction and death for the enemies of true Islam, so be it. . . . Seeing Islam as the basis of a political system touching every aspect of life, fundamentalists are totalitarian. Whatever the problem, "Islam is the solution." . . . Fundamentalists are revolutionary in outlook, extremist in behavior, totalitarian in ambition. . . . Like communism and fascism, [Islam] offers a vanguard ideology; a complete program to improve man and create a new society; complete control over that society; and cadres, ready, even eager, to spill blood.

On the other side of the debate are Graham E. Fuller and Ian O. Lesser, authors of *A Sense of Siege: The Geopolitics of Islam and the West*, who challenge the notion that Islam is an "ideology." They maintain that, just as the West reflects a vast diversity of beliefs and values, "Islam [cannot] be treated as a single, cohesive, coherent, comprehensive, monolithic entity." Those who agree with Fuller and Lesser argue that ominous claims such as those offered by Huntington and Pipes only serve to reemphasize prevalent stereotypes of Muslims as religious "fanatics"—stereotypes that lead to incidents of anti-Arab violence in Western countries—and encourage non-Muslims to adopt an "us-versus-them" attitude toward Islam. In reality, asserts Muslim activist Amira Elazhary Sonbol, "Anyone looking for [old-fashioned] American values can find them in Islam. It stresses family unity, caring for your mother and father, as well as bringing up children in the faith."

Still, both Muslims and non-Muslims agree that some radical groups operating in the name of Islam have instigated acts of terrorism against Western nations. Osama bin Laden, a Saudi Arabian millionaire and supporter of radical Islamic groups, is suspected to be the mastermind and financier behind countless acts of anti-Western terrorism, including the 1998 bombings of two U.S. embassies in Africa. Oliver B. Revell, former senior FBI official in charge of counter-terrorist investigations, warns that Islamic militants "are ultimately committed to waging holy war, both in the Middle East and the world at large against all of their opposition. And that means us."

However, claims Middle East scholar Antony T. Sullivan, many Westerners neglect to consider what drives Islamic terrorism in the first place. If some Muslims are hostile toward the West, he contends, that hostility "has much to do with Western policy before and during the Gulf War, as well as long-standing American policy toward Israel and Lebanon." In fact, in the view of many Muslims—including Muslim-Americans—the United States pursues foreign policies that either neglect or antagonize followers of Islam. For example, U.S. attacks on Iraq, which were viewed by many Americans as necessary to counter dictator Saddam

Hussein, were seen by Muslims as an attack on innocent Muslim civilians.

Differing perspectives about an event's significance are common in the debate over how the religion of Islam is changing social and political systems throughout the world. In *Islam: Opposing Viewpoints*, an array of scholars, political analysts, and journalists offer contrasting views about Islam in the following chapters: Are the Values of Islam and the West in Conflict? What Is the Status of Women Under Islam? Does Islam Promote Terrorism? and What Policies Should the U.S. Take Toward Islam? The authors in this anthology examine conflicting perceptions of Islam's values and consider how these values affect Muslim societies and the West.

CHAPTER 1

Are the Values of Islam and the West in Conflict?

Chapter Preface

The Satanic Verses, a comic novel by British author Salman Rushdie, set off a furor upon its publication in 1989. The book—which has since been banned in over twenty countries—was seen by Muslims as a defamation of Islam because it called into question the veracity of the prophet Muhammad's decrees. Soon after the book was published, Iranian president Ayatollah Khomeini issued an edict condemning Rushdie to death, and the Iranian Khordad Foundation offered a $2.5 million award to anyone who would carry out Rushdie's murder. For nine years, Rushdie, an ex-Muslim who was born in India, lived like a fugitive. Then, in September 1998, the Iranian government lifted the edict, stating that it would no longer threaten Rushdie's life or assist anyone else in doing so.

For many, the reversal in Iran's policy had tremendous implications for the future of Islamic and Western relations. The resolution of the Rushdie affair was seen by several commentators as a sign that Islam was beginning to reach out to the West, after years of hostility to Western values. British Foreign Minister Robin Cook stated that Iran's 1998 statement announced "the opening of a new chapter in . . . relations [between Islam and the West]."

Yet not everyone is convinced that Islamic policy on Salman Rushdie has truly changed. As Daniel Pipes, author of *The Rushdie Affair: The Novel, the Ayatollah, and the West*, writes, "Fundamentalist Muslims around the world hold Ayatollah Khomeini in uniquely high regard; for them, the death sentence against Rushdie remains a shining legacy." According to Pipes, the view that Islam has grown more accepting of Western values—especially the value of free speech—is a "delusion." The subsequent chapter explores in further detail the question of whether Islamic and Western values are in conflict.

> "*Islam . . . seeks to impose uniformity of thought and feeling on the faithful, and to subjugate and ultimately destroy its non-adherents.*"

Islamic Values Are Incompatible with Western Values

Srdja Trifkovic

Srdja Trifkovic, executive director of the Lord Byron Foundation for Balkan Studies, argues in the following viewpoint that, contrary to what many Western politicians assert, Islamic and Western civilizations cannot peacefully coexist. According to Trifkovic, Islam is not merely a religion but a dogmatic regime whose intent is to take over the world and convert all non-adherents.

As you read, consider the following questions:

1. What evidence does Trifkovic provide that Muhammad, the prophet of Islam, advocated violence?
2. How did Islam turn its boundary with the world into a "war zone," as explained by the author?
3. What is the relationship between Islam and Nazism, in the author's opinion?

Reprinted from Srdja Trifkovic, "Multiculturalism and Islam." This article first appeared in the February 1999 issue of *Chronicles: A Magazine of American Culture*, a publication of The Rockford Institute (928 N. Main St., Rockford, IL 61103).

"Some say there is an inevitable clash between Western civilization and Western values, and Islamic civilizations and values. I believe this view is terribly wrong. False prophets may use and abuse any religion to justify whatever political objectives they have—even cold-blooded murder. Some may have the world believe that almighty God himself, the merciful, grants a license to kill. But that is not our understanding of Islam. . . . There are over 1,200 mosques and Islamic centers in the United States, and the number is rapidly increasing. The six million Americans who worship there will tell you there is no inherent clash between Islam and America. Americans respect and honor Islam."

And so, on September 21, 1998, at the United Nations, President [Bill] Clinton declared the quest by our ruling establishment for a "moderate Islam" officially over. If "six million Americans" believe in something, that in itself is taken as proof that their ideals include religious tolerance, kindness to strangers, and aversion to violence. Like the unicorn or phlogiston, however, "tolerant Islam" can be defined and visualized, but it cannot be made *real*. In the name of "diversity," we are required to praise alternative religions, but Islam itself cannot tolerate diversity without ceasing to be what it is.

To the ruling post-Christian elite, this notion is unbearable. Having no faith themselves (except the baby boomers' belief in their own uniqueness), they do not take Islam's faith seriously. Smugly observing the demise of Christian belief and culture on both sides of the Atlantic, they trust the combined efforts of television, the Big Mac, and the public education system to make little Muhammad and Azra into carbon copies of Johnny and Chelsea.

It may not work. Contrary to Mr. Clinton's "understanding of Islam," this peculiar creed has been synonymous with violence and intolerance since its earliest days. Like Bolshevism and Nazism, Islam is part religion and part ideology, and it seeks to impose uniformity of thought and feeling on the faithful, and to subjugate and ultimately to destroy its non-adherents.

The beginnings of [prophet] Muhammad's public career are little known to most Westerners. A non-Muslim reading the Koran, however, might conclude that Muhammad's career was marked by a long string of killings, armed robberies, and rape, interspersed by a series of inspired pronouncements of varying coherence. Outsiders—the Jews of Medinah, or Muhammad's Arabic kinsmen who were reluctant to accept his self-proclaimed divinity—could testify to his unique concepts of justice and mercy.

When, in A.D. 626, for instance, six of Muhammad's henchmen murdered an elderly Jew by the name of Abu Rafi in his sleep, they argued afterwards whose weapon had actually ended the victim's life. The prophet decided that the person who owned the sword that still had traces of food on it was entitled to the credit. Abu Rafi had just finished his dinner before falling asleep, and the fatal slash went through his stomach.

If Abu Rafi's murder was a kind of *Kristallnacht* [a massive, coordinated attack on Jews throughout the German Reich on November 9, 1938], Muhammad's attack against the tribe of Banu-'l-Mustaliq, later in that same year, was a decisive step towards *Endloesung* [the Nazi's "final solution" to the "problem" of the Jews' murder]. His followers slaughtered many tribesmen and looted thousands of their camels and sheep; they also kidnapped 500 of their women. The night after the battle, Muhammad and his brigands staged an orgy of rape. As one Abu Sa'id Khudri remembered, a slight problem needed to be resolved first: In order to obtain ransom from the surviving tribesmen, the Muslims had pledged not to violate their captives.

> We were lusting after women and chastity had become too hard for us, but we wanted to get the ransom money for our prisoners. So we wanted to use the *Azl* [*coitus interruptus*]. . . . We asked the Prophet about it and he said: "You are not under any obligation to stop yourselves from doing it like that."

The members of the last surviving Jewish tribe in Medinah, Banu Qurayzah, were even less fortunate. Muhammad offered the men conversion to Islam as an alternative to death; upon their refusal, all 900 were decapitated in front of their enslaved women and children. The women were subsequently raped; Muhammad chose as his concubine one Raihana Bint Amr, whose father and husband were both slaughtered before her eyes only hours earlier.

The "Paragon" of Moral Behavior

This same man is explicitly upheld by all Muslims everywhere—from Los Angeles to Sarajevo, from Marseilles to Chechnya—as the paragon of godly, morally impeccable behavior, to be admired and emulated until the end of time. The prevalence of his name among Muslim men is symbolic of the covenant. His behavior, and that of his followers, was sanctioned in Muhammad's prophetic revelation, and duly recorded in his holy book:

> And all married women are forbidden unto you *except* those captives whom your right hand possesses. It is a decree of Allah for you. Lawful unto you are all beyond those mentioned, so that you seek them with your wealth in honest wedlock, not debauchery. . . . [Koran 4:24]

Non-Muslims who look for mercy and compassion from these quarters will search in vain. Muhammad explicitly forbade his followers to make friends of Christians and Jews, and warned them of the sanction for disobedience: "He among you who taketh them for friends is one of them" (Koran 5:51). But as the marauders could derive no material benefit from corpses, the lives of the conquered could be spared if they agreed to pay a hefty tribute to the Muslims. In his own lifetime, Muhammad thus established the model for subsequent relations between Islamic conquerors and their Christian or Jewish subjects.

The option of conversion was always available, and to be on the right side of Allah—and of history, as it seemed for a long time—was not too demanding. God, the creator and sustainer of the world, rewarded all those who expressed their worship in prayer, almsgiving, and self-purification, and above all in unquestioning obedience to Muhammad. That "God is great, and that there is no God but God" was easily grasped by the nomadic tribes of the desert and, later, of the steppe.

Underdeveloped culturally and socially, the nomads had few theological and logical qualms about Muhammad's claim that he was the sole spokesman for the authentic "religion of Abraham," a religion that had been corrupted by Jews and Christian alike. Since Jerusalem was, for the time being, out of reach, Muhammad audaciously attributed to Abraham the founding of the old pagan sanctuary, the *Ka'bah*, which housed a piece of black meteoric rock that became the Muslims' holy of holies. Later, non-Arab converts would translate "the crude and casual assertions of the Prophet" into a coherent teaching.

Muslim Aggression

In late summer of 1998, two United States embassies in East Africa were the target of murderous bomb attacks by Islamic terrorist groups. After ordering two retaliatory missile attacks on installations presumed to be connected with militant Islamic extremism, President Clinton hastened to assure the American people that he has nothing against Islam, which he called "a religion of peace." In November 1998, Islamic militants reacted violently to the progress of peace talks between Israel and the Palestine Liberation Organization with a series of terrorist attacks on Israelis, apparently with the intention of provoking a severe reaction by Israel. Again, we were assured that, contrary to the widespread impression, Islam is a peace-loving religion. . . .

This naïve insouciance with respect to Muslim aggressiveness is possible only if one is determined to disregard both history and present-day experience. St. Paul warns—in another context, it is true—"If the trumpet give an uncertain sound, who shall prepare himself to the battle?" (I Corinthians 14:8). At an interfaith meeting in 1995 held in Aiken, South Carolina, Boston College professor Peter Kreeft called for an "ecumenical *jihad*." The "five kings of orthodoxy"—Roman Catholicism, Eastern Orthodoxy, evangelical Protestantism, conservative Judaism, and (presumably non-fundamentalist) Islam were to unite to defeat the virulent forces of secularism. Unfortunately for Professor Kreeft's metaphor, *jihad* is defined as "a holy war waged on behalf of Islam as a religious duty," or "a bitter strife or crusade undertaken in the spirit of a holy war," and this does not harmonize well with ecumenical fraternizing. If there is to be a *jihad* involving Muslims, Christians, and Jews, it will not be cooperative but confrontational, and it will not be very quiet or very comfortable for us other "peoples of the Book."

Harold O.J. Brown, *Chronicles*, February 1999.

Between Muhammad's death in A.D. 626 and the second siege of Vienna, just over a thousand years later, Islam expanded—at first rapidly, then intermittently—at the expense of everything and everyone in the way of its warriors. But Islamic models of culture and society—represented by the horsemen who swept across three continents in the decades after Muhammad's death—were unable to induce the heirs of Christian, Middle Eastern, and Indian civilizations to attune their values and ways of life to the true faith.

There have been times when some Muslim lands were fit for a civilized man to live in. Baghdad under Harun ar-Rashid in the eighth and early ninth centuries or Cordova under Abd ar-Rahman in the tenth come to mind, but these brief periods of civilization were based on the readiness to borrow from earlier cultures, to compile, translate, learn, and absorb—a bit like America before the closing of its mind. These cultural awakenings happened in spite of the spirit of Islam, which—unable to engender interesting ideas of its own—rejected others as a threat.

In subsequent centuries, cross-fertilization of elements from diverse regions and traditions became increasingly difficult: Islam was accepted or rejected in its entirety, regardless of local custom or tradition. An unprecedented rigidity was introduced into the relations between civilizations, reflecting the fundamental tenet of Islam—accurately restated a decade ago by Bosnia's president, Alija Izetbegovic, in his *Islamic Declaration*—that "there can be no peace between Islam and other forms of social and political organization."

The Muslim Onslaught on Christianity

Unleashed as the militant faith of a barbarian war-band, Islam turned its boundary with the outside world into a perpetual war zone. For a long time, the outcome of the onslaught was in doubt. The early attack on Christendom reached as far west as Tours, and almost enabled the Koran—in Gibbon's memorable phrase—to be "taught in the schools of Oxford" to a circumcised people. The last attempt in pre-modern times, going through the Balkans, took the sultan's janissaries more than half-way from Constantinople to Dover. On both occasions, the tide was checked, but its subsequent rolling back took decades, even centuries.

For the millions of Christians and Jews engulfed by the deluge, those were centuries of quiet desperation interrupted by the regular pangs of agony. The materially and culturally rich Christian civilization of Byzantium and its budding

Slavic offspring in Serbia and Bulgaria were reduced to *dhimmis*, "people of the Book," whose advantage over pagans was that their life and earthly goods were ostensibly safe for as long as they submitted to Islamic rule. That rule rested on the two pillars of Islamic ideology and political practice—*jihad* and *Shari'a*—that provided the quasi-legal framework for institutionalized oppression of the infidels.

The story of the non-Muslims' experiences under Islamic rule is as politically incorrect to tell, and therefore as little known in today's America, as the remarkable life of Muhammad himself. At first, the choice of the vanquished seemed to be not "Islam or death" but "Islam or super-tax," but over time *Shari'a* ensured the decline of Eastern Christianity, the sapping of the captives' vitality and capacity for renewal. The practice of *devshirme*, the annual "blood levy" of Christian boys to be trained as janissaries, and the spiking of infidels were among its more obvious consequences.

Five Centuries of Muhammadan Misrule

If any single factor made the Balkans what they are today—to take a newsworthy example—it was the ordeal of five centuries of Muhammadan misrule. Modern attempts by some apologists for Islam in the West—notably, one Noel Malcolm—to present the sordid *casino* of Ottoman overlordship in southeast Europe as "tolerant," or even enlightened, are as intellectually dishonest as they are factually insupportable. Bat Ye'or's *The Decline of Eastern Christianity Under Islam* gives the lie to that. To understand Islam's record with its non-adherents, one should compare it not to Judaism nor Christianity, but rather match it against modern totalitarian ideologies, notably Bolshevism and National Socialism. Each explicitly denied the legitimacy of any form of social, political, or cultural organization other than itself. [Fascist Soviet dictator Joseph] Stalin's *forma mentis* [mind-set] was different from that of [former Iranian leader Ayatollah] Khomeini only in quantity, not in quality. The latter's statement that the Muslims have no choice but to wage "holy war against profane governments" until the conquest of the world has been accomplished was [former Soviet Communist Party Secretary Nikita] Khrushchev's "We shall bury you" wrapped in green instead of red. "Peaceful coexistence" was but *jihad* under another name. Islam, communism, and Nazism sought an eschatological shortcut that would enable the initiated to bypass the predicament of a seemingly aimless existence, while explicitly replacing Christian grace with the gnostic mantras of "surrender" ("Islam"), "dialectical materialism," "*Volksgemeinschaft* [the people's community]."

Nazism was the least coherent of the three; but it was among the Nazis (most notably with the architect of the holocaust, Heinrich Himmler) that Islam found its most willing promoters and collaborators in the pre-multicultural Europe. Himmler's hatred of "soft" Christianity was equal to his liking for Islam, which he saw as a masculine, martial religion based on the SS [Schutzstaffel, a complex military organization at the heart of the German Nazi political and social revolution] qualities of blind obedience and readiness for self-sacrifice, untainted by compassion for one's enemies. (While Hitler did not think much of Himmler's neo-pagan mysticism, he was happy to let Islam become the "SS religion.") By creating an SS division composed of Bosnian Muslims, Himmler sought to enhance the links between Nazi Germany and the Islamic world. One of his closest aides, *Obergruppenführer* Gottlob Berger, stated that

> a link is created between Islam and National-Socialism on an open, honest basis. It will be directed in terms of blood and race from the North, and in the ideological-spiritual sphere from the East.

In his drive to recruit Muslims, Himmler enlisted the support of the Grand Mufti of Jerusalem, El Husseini, who went to the Nazi puppet state of Croatia in 1943 to encourage his Bosnian Muslim flock to fight for the Reich. More than 20,000 enlisted in the 13th SS Division, *Hanjar* (the Turkish curved sword). The number of Bosnian Muslim volunteers in Himmler's units reached 46,000 by September 1943. This exceeded the number of Bosnian Muslims serving with Tito's Partisans and Croatian Ustašas together.

Half a century later, post-Christian "liberal democracy" expects to neuter Islam by reducing it to yet another humanistic project in self-celebration. Foreign policy strategists in Washington pander to its geopolitical designs, throwing smaller Christian nations—Serbs and Greek Cypriots today, Bulgars and Greeks tomorrow—to the wolves, hoping to balance the books for half a century of America's "passionate attachment" in the Middle East. They do not seem to realize that such morsels will only whet the Islamic appetite, paving the way to a major confrontation in the next century.

One way to avoid this is to open the gates and give up, and Islam's proselytizers in the West are learning how to play the game. They act as if Islam were just another competitor in the marketplace of the secular political system, without giving up their ultimate claims and objectives. Islam enters the new millennium with a strong hand. For starters, it is "nonwhite," non-European, and non-Christian, which makes it a natural ally of the ruling Western elites. At the same time, it has an inherent advantage over Clinton, [Tony] Blair, [German Chancellor Gerhard] Schröder, and [Jacques] Chirac, who are unable to generate an emotional response among the *hoi polloi* for their tepid ideology of multicultural mediocrity. It also has an advantage over most established Christian denominations, since the latter are no longer even "the Tory Party at Prayer" but—at best—"the Social Workers at Therapy." Richly endowed with petro-dollars, Islam's public relations front will use the symbols and vocabulary of the Dominant Tendency, and wait for its implosion.

Islam should not be blamed for being what it is, nor should its adherents be condemned for maintaining their traditions: Luther would say that they *kann nicht anders* [cannot be any different]. We should not hate it, nor ban it. We should, however, blame ourselves for refusing to acknowledge the facts of the case, and failing to take stock of our options. Those who have lost their own faith have little right to point a finger at those who uphold theirs.

In the present state of Western weakness, this process may well lead further millions to the conclusion that we should all become Muslims, since our goose is cooked anyway, spiritually and demographically. Those of us who do not cherish that prospect should at least demand that our rulers present that option fairly and squarely. To pretend—as Mr. Clinton does—that Islam is rather like Episcopalianism is plainly stupid or deeply dishonest. In view of the source, it is probably both.

*"Those who contrast Islamic civilization
or culture with 'our' modern Western
culture conveniently slip into an 'us and
them' mentality that . . . implies a 'static,
retrogressive them' and a 'dynamic,
progressive us.'"*

Islamic Values Are Compatible with Western Values

John L. Esposito

In the viewpoint that follows, John L. Esposito contends that there is no inherent clash between the values of Islam and those of Western civilization. In contrast to the popular wisdom that equates Islam with "fundamentalism," he writes, only a small minority of Muslims advocate violence, oppression, and authoritarianism. Islam is not a dangerous ideology, he asserts, but simply a religion that is not so different from Christianity and Judaism. Esposito, professor of religion and international affairs and director of the Center for Muslim-Christian Understanding at Georgetown University, is the author of *The Islamic Threat: Myth or Reality?* and *Islam: The Straight Path.*

As you read, consider the following questions:

1. What parallels does Esposito draw between Islam, Christianity, and Judaism?
2. What is the fundamental question facing contemporary Muslims, in the author's opinion?
3. What challenges does contemporary Islam pose for followers of Judaism and Christianity, according to Esposito?

Excerpted from John Esposito, "Islam and Christianity Face to Face," *Commonweal*, January 31, 1997, ©1997 Commonweal Foundation. Reprinted with permission. For subscriptions, call toll-free: 1-888-495-6755.

According to some, Islam and the West are on a political, demographic, and religio-cultural collision course. Past images of a Christian West turning back threatening Muslim armies are conjured up and linked to current political as well as demographic realities. Immigrants and immigration have become an explosive political issue in Europe and America.

If the 1980s were dominated by fear of "other Irans" or of underground terrorist groups, the emergence of Islam's "quiet revolution" has increased fears of political Islam. Its global force is now seen not only in the Islamic Republics of Iran, Sudan, and Afghanistan, but also in the emergence of Islamists as effective political and social actors in Turkey, Egypt, Jordan, Lebanon, Kuwait, Yemen, Pakistan, Bangladesh, Malaysia, and Indonesia.

Governments in the Middle East, both Arab states and Israel, play on such fears, warning of the dangers of "fundamentalism," domestically and internationally. Often their appeals conveniently obscure their own domestic political, economic, and social problems and causes for opposition and instability. The "fundamentalist" threat, described monolithically and equated solely with radicalism and terrorism, becomes a convenient pretext for crushing political opposition, nonviolent as well as violent, and backing away from previous commitments to democratization or greater political participation. For example, Tunisia's Zeine Abedin Ben Ali used such an excuse to "decapitate" his Islamic opposition (the Renaissance party which had emerged as the leading opposition in elections), as well as to silence secular opposition and thus win the elections of 1993 with 99.91 percent of the vote. With the end of the cold war and the threat of communism, a similar mission with a new threat, "Islamic fundamentalism," has become a primary excuse for Israel and Egypt to attract foreign aid or excuse human rights records of abuses. Fear of fundamentalists coming to power has often influenced European and American attitudes toward Turkey, Bosnia, Chechniya, Central Asia and, more broadly, the promotion of democratization in the Muslim world.

At the same time the record of Islamic experiments in Iran, Sudan, Pakistan, and, most recently, Afghanistan has reinforced fears of the export of terrorism. Reports of the forced veiling and seclusion of women, militant attacks against Christians in Egypt and Sudan, and discrimination against the Bahai in Iran and the Ahmadiyya in Pakistan exacerbate concerns about the rights of women and minorities. While many modern Muslim states granted equality of citizenship to all regardless of religious faith, the contemporary resurgence has resurrected pressures to reimplement classical Islamic laws which inform traditional attitudes and values that have remained operative in the minds and outlooks of many traditionally minded Muslims. Legal change implemented or imposed from the top down by a minority elite has not in many cases significantly changed popular culture and values.

An "Us and Them" Mentality

In recent years, there are those who speak of a clash of civilizations, a clash between Islam and "our" modern secular (or Judaeo-Christian) democratic values and culture. Those who contrast Islamic civilization or culture with "our" modern Western culture conveniently slip into an "us and them" mentality that obscures the diversity of both sides, and implies a "static, retrogressive them" and a "dynamic, progressive us." Several things should be kept in mind. The history of religions demonstrates that all three Abrahamic faiths (as indeed all religions) change; the issue is not change but degrees of change. All three traditions have within them divergent orientations: orthodox, conservative, reformist, fundamentalist, "secularist," etc. Judaism and Christianity, responding to pressing modern political, social, economic or cultural challenges/realities, experienced their reformations, but with diverse responses that continue to be reflected in their differing communities. For example, think of the vast diversity that exists between Orthodox and Reform Jews, Southern Baptist and Unitarian Christians on issues ranging from evolution to abortion.

Islam is experiencing, sometimes in similar and sometimes in dissimilar ways, the tensions and conflicts that accompany the interactions between tradition and change. The West, and Judaism and Christianity, experienced centuries-long struggles as a result of the political revolutions that accompanied the emergence of modern states and societies to the Reformation (which included warfare as well as theological disputation). Islam and Muslim communities have been severely limited by a lack of freedom and autonomy, first because of European colonialism and more recently, in many countries, by authoritarian governments. As with the Western experience, this political, social, and religio-cultural reformation or revolution is at times one of radical change whose experiments and progress can in the short term degenerate into violent revolution and radicalism, provoked by both political and religious authoritarianism and demagoguery.

Most Muslims are not Islamic political activists. In fact, such activists constitute only a minority, albeit a significant minority. Moreover, we must distinguish between a violent minority, bent upon the overthrow of governments, and a majority that, given the opportunity, will work within the system to bring about change. Even more difficult, of course, is distinguishing between legitimate and illegitimate uses of violence. When are revolutions just? When is violence or warfare defensive rather than offensive? When is it just or unjust?

Islam in the West

The remarkable growth of Islam in Europe and America, where it is now the second- or third-largest religion, has raised fears about whether Muslims can be loyal citizens and even whether they will bring "fundamentalist" violence to the West. The World Trade Center bombing as well as bombings in Paris and France help to feed such fears. France has insisted on integration, not multiculturalism. Muslims have experienced levels of discrimination in society and the media in Europe and America that would simply not be tolerated by Christians and Jews.

Islam, like Christianity and Judaism, is a religion that provides a framework of faith and meaning that has transformed lives and societies. At the same time, again like Judaism and Christianity, it has been used or abused to justify violence and oppression. We can speak equally about militant Judaism and Christianity as we can about militant Islam. Part of our problem of interpretation is that when a Jewish extremist murdered Muslims at prayer in the Hebron mosque or assassinated Prime Minister Itzhak Rabin, or when Christian extremists, calling themselves the army of God, blew up an abortion clinic, we reflexively distinguished between the mainstream faith of Jews and Christians and the twisted use of religion by fanatics. Making an equivalent distinction with regard to Islam does not regularly occur. Similarly, while some do not object to the mixing of religion and politics in Israel, Eastern Europe, or Latin America (liberation theology), they will do so in a blanket way when it comes to Islam.

The Need for Dialogue Between Islam and the West

The West has to understand Islam; not because Islam is the next great threat, but because Islam contains so many ideas and moral values that the West, for all its rampant secularism, still shares. The West must also recognise the diversity of Muslim experiences across the world. Muslim societies do not only suffer from "Islamic" problems; they suffer the same problems long familiar in the West: political, economic, ecological, social and moral development. As such, these are shared human experiences and the beneficial resolutions: in science, technology, medicine, education should also be shared equitably. If Western nations believe in the value of their defining concepts—individualism, liberalism, constitutionalism, human rights, equality, liberty, the rule of law, democracy, free markets, and the separation of church and state—then they will have to be shared through sympathetic dialogue, not forced upon others. The idea of contending world views which define the good states from the bad states will have to be scrapped.

I. Bruce Watson, *Insight*, May 1997.

As Jews faced the challenges of preserving a sense of identity, community, and faith within an American society dominated by Christian culture and values, Muslims today as a religious minority face a similar challenge within a Judaeo-Christian or secular America. Real understanding can begin when we, the majority, come to realize that, despite our differences, there is a common Judaeo-Christian-Islamic heritage shared by all the children of Abraham, and that Islam is not a "foreign" or Middle Eastern religion any more than

Judaism and Christianity. The Muslim presence in America spans centuries, not decades, and with a population of at least from 4 to 6 million, Muslims are indeed "us." The failures of our educational system to make us aware of these facts and our media's presentation of present Islam and Muslims only through "headline events" have distorted or obscured these realities.

Islamic Reform

This is an exceptionally dynamic and fluid period in Muslim history. Diverse voices in the Muslim world are grappling with issues from scriptural criticism and exegesis, modernism, democracy, and pluralism to women's rights and family values. The voices for substantive change are a minority and themselves divided, much as was the case, for example, in Roman Catholicism in the late nineteenth and the first half of the twentieth century regarding modernism, pluralism, biblical criticism, and dissent. The days of excommunication, silencing, or banishment, the index of forbidden books, the easy consignment of "others" to hell, the struggle between the religious establishment and the laity may be in large part gone, but are not all that far behind us. For Muslims, who struggle with similar problems in many societies where political participation and freedom of expression have been restricted, and authoritarianism, patriarchy, and violence all too common, the battle can be especially contentious.

The fundamental question or issue for contemporary Muslims, one which affects Muslim-Christian relations as well, is the direction of Islamic revival or reform. Will it simply be a process of restoration of classical law, or will it be one of reformation: a reformulation of Islamic law that distinguishes between the immutable and the mutable, between that which is divine and that which is the product of human interpretation? For believers everywhere, this is an all-too-familiar question.

Contemporary Islam challenges us all to know and understand the richness and diversity of the Muslim experience. Followers of Christianity and Judaism are specifically challenged to recall or to become aware of the faith of Islam, to acknowledge their Muslim brothers and sisters as children of Abraham. Muslim governments are challenged to be more responsive to popular demands for political liberalization and greater popular participation, to tolerate rather than repress opposition movements (including Islamic organizations and parties), and to build viable, democratic institutions. At the same time, new Islamic governments and movements are challenged to demonstrate by word and action that they acknowledge the rights of others, that pluralism and human rights are not valued only when Muslims seek access to power but also when they are in power. Self-criticism and the denunciation of religious extremism, intolerance, and authoritarianism are the only means by which Islamist claims can be credible.

Western powers are challenged to stand by the democratic values they embody and to recognize authentic populist movements and the right of the people to determine populist movements and the right of the people to determine the nature of their governments and leadership, whether they choose a secular or a more Islamically oriented path.

And finally, as Christians and Jews, or their secular counterparts, view the changing specter of Islam, they need to remember their own histories. Moreover, they must seek to understand before they judge, not to excuse, but to be sure that their judgments, which have implications both internationally and domestically, are fair and informed.

> *"There is one common feature of Islamism as it assumes power: an irresistible leaning toward authoritarianism."*

Islam Presents an Obstacle to Democracy

Martin Kramer

In the subsequent viewpoint, Martin Kramer, director of the Moshe Dayan Center for Middle Eastern and African Studies at Tel Aviv University, asserts that Islam does not support the principles of democracy. He claims that the true agenda of Islamic movements is to gain power, establish authoritarian rule, and repress dissent. Based on their belief that they are implementing the will of God, Kramer maintains, Islamic fundamentalists are trying to dominate the West.

As you read, consider the following questions:
1. How does Kramer define "ideological Islam"?
2. What are the ways by which Islamists pursue power, according to the author?
3. As stated by Kramer, what is the role of the Islamic state?

Excerpted from Martin Kramer, "Ballots and Bullets: Islamists and the Relentless Drive for Power," *Harvard International Review*, Spring 1997. Reprinted with permission.

Will the real political Islam stand up? In July 1996, the leader of Turkey's Islamist Refah (Welfare) Party, Necmettin Erbakan, emerged as prime minister in a coalition government. Despite Erbakan's past rhetoric, his government seemed to act cautiously, respecting the secular institutions of state, preserving Turkey's NATO membership, and even maintaining relations with Israel. Was this not proof that Islamists could be trusted with power and its prerogatives?

Then in September 1996, the Taleban, another Islamist movement, overran the Afghan capital of Kabul. In a spasm of moral rectitude, the Taleban banned women from the workplace and insisted that they veil themselves in public. The zealots ordered men to grow beards and burned Western films outside theaters. Was this not the genuine face of Islamism, pockmarked by intolerance for other Muslims and hatred of Western ways?

These two very different images of political Islam once again produced confusion in the West, and the sense that no meaningful generalizations could be made about Islamist movements at all. Experts, whose stock-in-trade is drawing distinctions, once again hammered away at the theme of "diversity": these movements arise in different circumstances; they are driven by different forces; each is an island unto itself. Social scientists tweaked their intricate systems of categorization to accommodate the latest variations in Ankara and Kabul. And policymakers were not far behind, formulating more litmus tests that would distinguish Islamist "moderates" from Islamist "extremists."

At some level, of course, they are right: Islamist movements are not all alike. Islam is a world religion. One billion believers inhabit an area stretching from the African shores of the Atlantic to the Asian islands of the Pacific. Muslims share a faith and its myths, but their histories diverge dramatically. Islamists, like their co-religionists, are made by these histories even as they make them.

Consider, for example, Turkey and Afghanistan, the settings of Islamism's latest gains. Turkey is the front door of Islam, a country surrounded by seas and straits, open to Europe. Afghanistan is Islam's back door, a landlocked country of narrow mountain passes, remote even from its neighbors.

The impact of the West—of modernity and secularism—has been very different in each country: profound in Turkey, superficial in Afghanistan. So it should come as no surprise that Turkey's Islamists feel at home in jacket and tie, and are masters of parliamentary jousting. Afghanistan's Islamists are bearded and turbaned warlords whose claim to legitimacy is the rifle—and whose sole concession to modernity is that the rifle is automatic. Islamists are not above history, and history accounts for an intrinsic diversity in Islamism. In this sea of differences, it would be surprising if Islamist movements shared anything at all.

But they do. In the preoccupation with the unique predicament of each Islamist state and movement, it is easy to lose sight of the essentials of Islamism itself, and to underestimate the challenge every form of Islamism poses to the West.

The Pursuit of Power

Political Islam is the preferred term of the policymakers, but it misses the point. The usual Muslim view has been that Islam does not allow the distinction between the temporal and the sacred, between religion and the state, that has been the defining feature of the secular West since the Enlightenment. In a profound sense, Islam has always been political, and it is invoked and manipulated for political purposes by nearly all regimes and their opponents. In Egypt both Anwar Sadat and those who assassinated him in 1981 used Islam politically, to very different ends; so too do the Saudi monarchy and its opposition today. Political Islam, then, may well be a tautology; at best, it is a banal description of the way Islam is believed and practiced by the great majority of Muslims.

Ideological Islam, now most often called Islamism, is something very different, much narrower in its appeal, and much more focused in its objectives and methods. Islamists turn Islam from a traditional mix of faith and politics into a total ideological system, a modern "ism." The translation of Islam into an ideology began more than a century ago, in the actions and writings of Sayyid Jamal al-Din "al-Afghani," a preacher and activist whose teachings had an impact across the Islamic world. In Arab lands, two Egyptians refined these ideas into a program: Hasan al-Banna, who founded the Muslim Brotherhood in the 1920s, and Sayyid Qutb, the Brotherhood's chief ideologue. In the Indian subcontinent, Abu'l 'Ala Mawdudi made a crucial intellectual contribution. And in Iran, Ayatollah Khomeini adapted this ideology to Shi'ism and then galvanized a movement that carried Islamism to power for the first time.

Islam Is Not Democratic

Statements by fundamentalist spokesmen from widely dispersed countries suggest an open disdain for popular sovereignty. Ahmad Nawfal, a Muslim Brother from Jordan, says that "[i]f we have a choice between democracy and dictatorship, we choose democracy. But if it's between Islam and democracy, we choose Islam." Hadi Hawang of Partai Islam Se-Malaysia (PAS) in Malaysia makes the same point more bluntly: "I am not interested in democracy. Islam is not democracy, Islam is Islam." Or, in the famous (if not completely verified) words of Ali Belhadj, a leader of Algeria's Islamic Salvation Front (FIS), "When we are in power, there will be no more elections because God will be ruling."

Daniel Pipes, *National Interest*, Fall 1995.

In the ideology devised by these thinkers and activists, Islam is much more than the final revelation, come from above to supersede Judaism and Christianity. It is hailed as the final system, come to supersede capitalism and communism as the true key to power in this world. There is nothing abstract about this idea of power. It is worldly, temporal power, of the kind Muslims enjoyed for the first millennium of Islam. Throughout that period, Muslims ruled vast empires, led the world in cultural innovation, and mastered the sciences. Now many Muslims ask why it is that foreigners have come to dominate them, and why the Islamic world is poor and unproductive, left far behind by the West, and, increasingly, by the Far East as well.

The Islamist Answer

The Islamist answer is simple: Muslims have fallen away from the essence of Islam, personified by the example of the Prophet Muhammad and codified in Islamic law, the *shari'a*, a code based on direct revelation from God. Muslims will remain in their wretched state until they purify themselves by reinstituting this law. If Muslims do as the Prophet did—if they are willing to implement the law of Islam without apology and rely on their faith in revelation to defy the great powers of the day—then this world will be theirs.

The first step is repossession of the state. Islamism is not inward asceticism. It does seek to promote inner transformation, but with a political rather than a spiritual purpose: to fortify believers to make the sacrifices demanded by the pursuit of power. Nor is Islamism social service. Of course Islamist movements do seek to build social bases, and some are famous for distributing medicines and schoolbooks. But for Islamists, social transformation is never an end in itself because civil society is weak, and its conquest is no guarantee that Islamists will prevail.

The only locus of real power is the state, buttressed by the bureaucracy and the army. Only the state has the material means and the coercive force to Islamize itself and society. Islamism, therefore, cannot remain content to function as a social movement. To fulfill its destiny, it must capture the state and rule. From the very beginnings of Islamism, political power has been the obsession of every Islamist thinker, leader, and movement.

By Any Means Necessary

The most pressing question that has faced Islamists has been how to pursue rulership. The rule of thumb here is that Islamist movements usually follow what looks to their leaders like the path of least resistance. They are not committed to any one strategy in the pursuit of their ends, and any means are legitimate as long as they are in accordance with Islamic law, the *shari'a*. This law is not pacifist. It sanctions violence for the legitimate purposes of defending Muslims and establishing the rule of Islam. This explains why Islamist movements have slipped so readily into violence whenever it has seemed like a shortcut to power. In such circumstances, the use of force is not deemed a deviation, but an obligation.

Islamist movements may choose from a wide variety of approaches in their pursuit of power. In a system that is comparatively open, Islamists may form political parties and compete for voters, as they have in Turkey and Jordan. In a system that is closed but betrays a lack of resolve at its core, Islamists often undertake violent and even revolutionary acts in their attempt to claim power. This was the case in Iran of the Shah; Islamists (erroneously) read this to be the case in Algeria. One particularly striking feature of many Islamist movements has been their simultaneous resort to political and violent means, through the creation of political and military wings—the classic strategy of the Muslim Brotherhood throughout the Arab world. The mix of means differs widely from setting to setting, but the basic instinct of all Islamist movements is the same: follow the shortest road to power.

Given this indifference to means, Islamists cannot be divided into the fixed categories of "moderate" and "extremist." The movements that have political and military wings—that simultaneously use bullets and ballots—are impossible to classify. Other movements, even when they desist from violence, rarely renounce it, and almost never denounce other Islamists who do use it. For them, violence still remains a legitimate option, whether or not it is exercised.

If the line between "moderate" and "extremist" is drawn not just between means but between ideas, no Islamist movement fits neatly into either category. For example, most Islamists favor economic policies that would be regarded in the West as "moderate," yet they favor social policies, especially with regard to women, that would be regarded as "extremist." Finally, Islamist movements are also constantly moving in response to changing circumstances. A "moderate" Islamist ally can rapidly become an "extreme" Islamist enemy, as did the mujahideen [holy fighters] of the Afghan war, who went from Cold War allies of the United States to conspirators intent upon blowing up Manhattan skyscrapers and traffic tunnels. In short, the efforts of social scientists and governments to pigeonhole Islamists have created immense blind spots, concealing the complexities of Islamist choices.

Islamism in Power

The essentials of Islamism come into clearer focus wherever Islamism is in power. Here, too, there is variety, because not all of the Islamists in power exercise power to the same degree. In Turkey, Islamists must share it with secular coalition partners, while a vigilant army watches from the wings. In Sudan, they have far greater scope, but still have a military junta as partners. In Afghanistan, they have not yet consolidated their hold over the country. Only Iran may be described as an Islamist state in the full sense.

Yet there is one common feature of Islamism as it assumes power: an irresistible leaning toward authoritarianism. The explanation, again, lies in Islamist thought: Islamists share the idea that God, not the people, is sovereign, and that obedience to God, not the rights of man, must be the governing principles of a just state. The role of the Islamic state is not to legislate the will of the people, but to implement the will of God.

Islamist states have created different institutions to achieve this end. In Iran, for example, an elected parliament implements the law, an acknowledgment that there are several different ways to interpret the law, that they are all legitimate, and that only a representative body can choose among them. Nevertheless, parliamentarians must first have a proven commitment to Islam, and so they must be screened prior to candidature. This screening board disqualified 40 percent of the candidates for the 1996 parliamentary elections. Since even this cannot guarantee the right outcome, the choices of the parliament are subordinated yet again to a council of "guardians," whose task is to reject any legislation that stretches Islamic law too far. To prevent the emergence of an organized opposition, political parties are not permitted inside or outside the parliament. In short, the Islamists have allowed some open space for debate—only among themselves.

In Sudan, the process of implementation is much simpler. An assembly, more selected than elected, rubberstamps the decrees of the military junta, working hand-in-hand with its Islamist mention, Hasan al-Turabi. Turabi, arguing that Sudan faces a state of emergency, has blocked every avenue of dissent by banning political parties and muzzling the press. Sudan, unlike Iran, was once a democratic polity, and Islamists first organized in an atmosphere of relative political freedom.

Having now seized power, they have worked systematically to exclude all others as they impose their program.

Some Western apologists for Islamism—and they are numerous in academe—have argued that the dismal record of Iran and Sudan should not be counted against Islamism itself. They point out that the Islamists came to power in Iran by revolution and in Sudan by coup, and that neither is conducive to the building of pluralistic, democratic institutions. Were an Islamist movement to be carried to power by free elections, they argue, the results would be different.

But power is not always exercised in the way it is acquired. In the middle of this century, free elections brought to power the worst of the totalitarians, who then preyed upon the very democracies that empowered them. Power is exercised in the way it is envisioned, not acquired, and it is a conception of power that explains why both the Iranian and Sudanese Islamists—separated by language, sect, and historical experience—have produced regimes from the same mold. Their concept of power, developed in the shared corpus of Islamist thought, does not admit that power can be shared, any more than religious truth can be shared. The truth is indivisible; so, too, must be the rule of truth. For anyone who has read the Islamist theoreticians, it cannot come as a surprise that Islamism in actual power has always been authoritarian. So long as Islamism rests on the idea of divine sovereignty, it cannot be otherwise.

Islamists and the West

One highly developed aspect of Islamist thought is an antagonism toward the West. Islamism makes its promises of Muslim power in a world dominated by the modern West. The power Islamists seek cannot be acquired without diminishing the power of the West, and when the West does not cede it, Islamists do not shy from confrontation.

This is a "clash of civilizations" many in the West understandably wish to avoid, but this wish often leads to an underestimation of the Islamists' own determination. In a recent article in *Foreign Policy*, an author has written that "outside of the Islamic world, most Islamic fundamentalists have no ambition other than the most anodyne desire for security." Therefore, "Islamic fundamentalism ought to matter no more to the non-Muslim world than Quebecois nationalism matters to Thailand." The first statement is blithely innocent of what the Islamists themselves put forward as their ambition. The latter displays a breathtaking ignorance of the history, and memory, of Islam's relations with the West.

"We might not have the actual power the United States has," says Ayatollah Fadlallah, the guide of Lebanon's Hezbullah, "but we had the power previously and we now have the foundations to develop that power in the future." This is the Islamist ambition: power on a great scale. Islam indeed had such power: during the first millennium of Islam, there was no moment when some part of Europe was not under Muslim rule or threat of conquest. In the eighth century, the forces of Islam crossed the Pyrenees; in the seventeenth, they besieged the gates of Vienna. Today, the tables have been turned, and nonbelievers exercise many times the power of Muslim believers. The Islamist ambition is to take that power back.

The Islamist Ambition

Power must be reclaimed from non-Muslim minorities within Islamic societies, which still sometimes exercise a disproportionate influence. It must be recovered from the Jews now collected in the state of Israel, where they intimidate Muslims with their military might. And it must be subtracted from the Western powers, led by the United States, which dominate the Islamic world through instruments as diverse as movies, news networks, banks, and cruise missiles.

Not surprisingly, the Islamists' "most anodyne desire for security" has not ended at Islam's shores. Over the past ten years, it has inspired the World Trade Center bombing in New York, several attempts to lay siege to Paris by bombing sprees, the death warrant on British author Salman Rushdie, and massive car bombings that leveled entire buildings in Buenos Aires. This is clearly a conflict that Islamists are prepared to carry beyond the terrain of Islam.

The extent of Islamist ambition, to read and hear the Islamists, is far-reaching. "Islam is regenerating, the two superpowers are degenerating," claims an Egyptian Islamist. "Islam is the power of the future, inheriting the two superpowers in the present." True, they admit, the West seems omnipotent. But it also trades many of the basic tools of its dominance: tanks, fighter planes, missiles, chemicals, and even bits and pieces of nuclear technology. After all, the United States provided Iran with TOW [tube-launched, optically tracked wire command-link guided] anti-tank missiles in exchange for hostages; it provided the Afghan mujahideen with Stingers to fight the Soviets. With rope bought from the West, Muslims might be able to bind Western hands. At some level, then, an Islamist state will demonstrate pragmatism, if only to acquire what it needs to grow strong.

"Neither Islam nor its culture is the major obstacle to political modernity, even if undemocratic rulers sometimes use Islam as their excuse."

Islam Does Not Present an Obstacle to Democracy

Robin Wright

Robin Wright, a global-affairs correspondent for the *Los Angeles Times* and former Middle East correspondent for the *Sunday Times* of London, challenges the belief that Islam and democracy are incompatible. In the viewpoint that follows, she contends that the tenets of Islam can be interpreted to support a modern, democratic society. Wright, author of *Sacred Rage: The Wrath of Militant Islam* and *In the Name of God: The Khomeini Decade*, explains how Islamic reformers are working to clarify the concept of an Islamic democracy and implement democratic ideals within the Muslim world.

As you read, consider the following questions:

1. As stated by Wright, what are the two pillars upon which Abdul Karim Soroush's advocacy of democracy rests?
2. What type of Islamic system does reformer Rachid al-Ghannouchi advocate, as cited by Wright?
3. How is the Islamic Reformation similar to the Christian Reformation, in the author's opinion?

Excerpted from Robin Wright, "Islam and Liberal Democracy: Two Visions of Reformation," *Journal of Democracy*, vol. 7, no. 2 (1996), pp. 64–75, © The Johns Hopkins University Press and National Endowment for Democracy. Reprinted with permission.

Of all the challenges facing democracy in the 1990s, one of the greatest lies in the Islamic world. Only a handful of the more than four dozen predominantly Muslim countries have made significant strides toward establishing democratic systems. Among this handful—including Albania, Bangladesh, Jordan, Kyrgyzstan, Lebanon, Mali, Pakistan, and Turkey—not one has yet achieved full, stable, or secure democracy. And the largest single regional bloc holding out against the global trend toward political pluralism comprises the Muslim countries of the Middle East and North Africa.

Yet the resistance to political change associated with the Islamic bloc is not necessarily a function of the Muslim faith. Indeed, the evidence indicates quite the reverse. Rulers in some of the most antidemocratic regimes in the Islamic world—such as Brunei, Indonesia, Iraq, Oman, Qatar, Syria, and Turkmenistan—are secular autocrats who refuse to share power with their brethren.

Overall, the obstacles to political pluralism in Islamic countries are not unlike the problems earlier faced in other parts of the world: secular ideologies such as Ba'athism in Iraq and Syria, Pancasila in Indonesia, or lingering communism in some former Soviet Central Asian states brook no real opposition. Ironically, many of these ideologies were adapted from the West; Ba'athism, for instance, was inspired by the European socialism of the 1930s and 1940s. Rigid government controls over everything from communications in Saudi Arabia and Brunei to foreign visitors in Uzbekistan and Indonesia also isolate their people from democratic ideas and debate on popular empowerment. In the largest and poorest Muslim countries, moreover, problems common to developing states, from illiteracy and disease to poverty, make simple survival a priority and render democratic politics a seeming luxury. Finally, like their non-Muslim neighbors in Asia and Africa, most Muslim societies have no local history of democracy on which to draw. As democracy has blossomed in Western states over the past three centuries, Muslim societies have usually lived under colonial rulers, kings, or tribal and clan leaders.

In other words, neither Islam nor its culture is the major obstacle to political modernity, even if undemocratic rulers sometimes use Islam as their excuse. In Saudi Arabia, for instance, the ruling House of Saud relied on Wahhabism, a puritanical brand of Sunni Islam, first to unite the tribes of the Arabian Peninsula and then to justify dynastic rule. Like other monotheistic religions, Islam offers wide-ranging and sometimes contradictory instruction. In Saudi Arabia, Islam's tenets have been selectively shaped to sustain an authoritarian monarchy.

In Iran, the revolution that overthrew the shah in 1979 put a new spin on Shi'ite traditions. The Iranian Shi'ite community had traditionally avoided direct participation by religious leaders in government as demeaning to spiritual authority. The upheaval led by Ayatollah Ruhollah Khomeini thus represented not only a revolution in Iran, but also a revolution within the Shi'ite branch of Islam. The constitution of the Islamic Republic, the first of its kind, created structures and positions unknown to Islam in the past.

Yet Islam, which acknowledges Judaism and Christianity as its forerunners in a single religious tradition of revelation-based monotheism, also preaches equality, justice, and human dignity—ideals that played a role in developments as diverse as the Christian Reformation of the sixteenth century, the American and French revolutions of the eighteenth century, and even the "liberation theology" of the twentieth century. Islam is not lacking in tenets and practices that are compatible with pluralism. Among these are the traditions of *ijtihad* (interpretation), *ijma* (consensus), and *shura* (consultation).

Diversity and Reform

Politicized Islam is not a monolith; its spectrum is broad. Only a few groups, such as the Wahhabi in Saudi Arabia, are in fact fundamentalist. This term, coined in the early twentieth century to describe a movement among Protestant Christians in the United States, denotes passive adherence to a literal reading of sacred scripture. By contrast, many of today's Islamic movements are trying to adapt the tenets of the faith to changing times and circumstances. In their own way, some even resemble Catholic "liberation theology" movements in their attempts to use religious doctrines to transform temporal life in the modern world. The more accurate word for such Muslim groups is "Islamist." The term is growing in popularity in Western academic and policy-making circles, since it better allows for the forward-looking, interpretive, and often innovative stances that such groups assume as they seek to bring about a reconstruction of the social order.

The common denominator of most Islamist movements, then, is a desire for change. The quest for something different is manifested in a range of activities, from committing acts of violence to running for political office. Reactive groups—motivated by political or economic insecurity, questions of identity, or territorial disputes—are most visible because of their aggressiveness. Extremists have manipulated, misconstrued, and even hijacked Muslim tenets. Similar trends have emerged in religions other than Islam: the words "zealot" and "thug" were coined long ago to refer, respectively, to Jewish and Hindu extremists. Contemporary Islamic extremists have committed acts of terrorism as far afield as Buenos Aires, Paris, and New York, and they have threatened the lives of writers whom they regard as blasphemous from Britain to Bangladesh.

At the opposite end of the spectrum are proactive individuals and groups working for constructive change. In Egypt, Islamists have provided health-care and educational facilities as alternatives to expensive private outlets and inadequate government institutions. In Turkey, they have helped to build housing for the poor and have generally strengthened civil society. In Lebanon, they have established farm cooperatives and provided systematically for the welfare of children, widows, and the poor. In Jordan, Yemen, Kuwait, and elsewhere, they have run for parliament. The specific motives vary from religiously grounded altruism to creating political power bases by winning hearts and minds. But in diverse ways, they are trying to create alternatives to ideas and systems that they believe no longer work.

Laying the Foundations for an Islamic Reformation

Less visible but arguably more important—to both Muslims and the world at large—is a growing group of Islamic reformers. While reactive and proactive groups address the immediate problems of Islam's diverse and disparate communities, the reformers are shaping thought about long-term issues. At the center of their reflections is the question of how to modernize and democratize political and economic systems in an Islamic context. The reformers' impact is not merely academic; by stimulating some of the most profound debate since Islam's emergence in the seventh century, they are laying the foundations for an Islamic Reformation.

The stirrings of reform within Islam today should not be compared too closely with the Christian Reformation of almost five hundred years ago. The historical and institutional differences between the two faiths are vast. Nonetheless, many of the issues ultimately addressed by the respective movements are similar, particularly the inherent rights of the individual and the relationship between religious and political authority.

The seeds of an Islamic Reformation were actually planted a century ago, but only among tiny circles of clerics and intellectuals whose ideas were never widely communicated to ordinary believers. At the end of the twentieth century, however, instant mass communications, improved education, and intercontinental movements of both people and ideas mean that tens of millions of Muslims are exposed to the debate. In the 1980s, interest in reform gained momentum as the secular ideologies that succeeded colonialism—mostly variants or hybrids of nationalism and socialism—failed to provide freedom and security to many people in the Muslim world. This sense of ferment has only grown more intense amid the global political upheaval of the post–Cold War world. Muslims now want political, economic, and social systems that better their lives, and in which they have some say.

The reformers contend that human understanding of Islam is flexible, and that Islam's tenets can be interpreted to accommodate and even encourage pluralism. They are actively challenging those who argue that Islam has a single, definitive essence that admits of no change in the face of time, space, or experience—and that democracy is therefore incompatible or alien. The central drama of reform is the attempt to reconcile Islam and modernity by creating a worldview that is compatible with both.

Two Middle Eastern philosophers symbolize the diverse origins of Islamist reformers and the breadth of their thought. Abdul Karim Soroush is a Shi'ite Muslim and a Persian from Iran. He is a media-shy academic who has experienced almost a generation of life inside an Islamic republic. Sheikh Rachid al-Ghannouchi is a Sunni Muslim and a Tunisian Arab. He is the exiled leader of Hezb al-Nahda (Party of the Renaissance), a movement intent on creating an Islamic republic in Tunisia. Over the past three years, Soroush and Ghannouchi have produced some of the most far-reaching work on the question of Islam and democracy.

Abdul Karim Soroush

Soroush supported Iran's 1979 revolution and took an active role in revising university curricula during its early years. Since then, however, he has articulated ideas that the regime considers highly controversial. Ranking officials such as Ayatollah Ali Khamenei, the successor to Ayatollah Khomeini, now Iran's Supreme Guide, have increasingly framed public remarks as implicit but unmistakeable responses to Soroush's articles and speeches. Some of Soroush's ideas amount to heresy in the regime's eyes, and the tenor of Khamenei's statements has become increasingly hostile. In a November 1995 address commemorating the 1979 U.S. Embassy takeover, Khamenei spent more time condemning Soroush's ideas than lambasting the United States or Israel.

The degree to which Soroush now frames the debate in Iran was revealed by two unusual events that took place in the autumn of 1995. At Tehran University, more than a hundred young members of Ansar (Helpers of the Party of God) physically attacked and injured Soroush as he attempted to give a special address that the Muslim Students' Association had invited him to deliver. Some among the two thousand students who had assembled to hear him were also injured. The attack then sparked a pro-Soroush demonstration on campus. A new law imposing severe penalties on anyone associating with critics and enemies of the Islamic Republic was widely thought to be aimed at undermining Soroush's growing support.

Educated in London and Tehran in both philosophy and

the physical sciences, Soroush has recently taught at the Institute for Human Research and at Tehran University's School of Theology. His columns have been the centerpiece of Kiyan (a Farsi word that can mean "foundation" or "universe"), a bimonthly magazine founded in 1991 primarily to air his views and the debate that they have sparked. For years he also gave informal talks at Tehran mosques that were usually packed by followers ranging from young clerics to regime opponents, intellectuals, political independents, and government technocrats. But in the fall of 1995, the government banned him from giving public lectures or instruction and from publishing. He has been effectively forced from public view, and his academic career in Iran has been ended.

Islam Supports the Principles of Democracy

Democracy is not an alien concept to Islam. When the Prophet of Islam died, he did not appoint any person or group of people to lead the Muslim society. The companions of the Prophet . . . were asked to convene in a house and elect a new leader, Abu Bakr. By not appointing a successor, Prophet Muhammad . . . clearly wanted to teach his followers that it is up to them to choose their leader. Therefore it is clear that the ruler in a Muslim society does not represent God Almighty but represents and serves the people who elect him. He serves at their pleasure and can be removed from office if he does not do a good job. Although Islam does not specify how these elections are to take place or the mechanism by which the ruler is made accountable to the people, Islam clearly forbids repression and oppression and advocates justice, freedom of religion, freedom of expression, and the freedom to criticize, or even oppose, the ruler. Islam is inherently democratic because it does not have a religious hierarchy or spokesperson. What Islam has is generations of religious scholars (*Ulama*), and Muslims are in effect free to choose whom to follow or *not to follow*.

Center for the Study of Islam and Democracy, Mission Statement. Available at http://www.islam-democracy.org/mission.htm.

Soroush's writings on three subjects are particularly relevant. At the top of the list is democracy. Although Islam literally means "submission," Soroush argues that there is no contradiction between Islam and the freedoms inherent in democracy. "Islam and democracy are not only compatible, their association is inevitable. In a Muslim society, one without the other is not perfect," he said in one of several interviews in Tehran and Washington, D.C., in 1994 and 1995.

His advocacy of democracy for the Islamic world rests on two pillars. First, to be a true believer, one must be free. Belief attested under threat or coercion is not true belief. And if a believer freely submits, this does not mean that he has sacrificed freedom. He must also remain free to leave his faith. The only real contradiction is to be free in order to believe, and then afterward to abolish that freedom. This freedom is the basis of democracy. Soroush goes further: the beliefs and will of the majority must shape the ideal Islamic state. An Islamic democracy cannot be imposed from the top; it is only legitimate if it has been chosen by the majority, including nonbelievers as well as believers.

Second, says Soroush, our understanding of religion is evolving. Sacred texts do not change, but interpretation of them is always in flux because understanding is influenced by the age and the changing conditions in which believers live. So no interpretation is absolute or fixed for all time and all places. Furthermore, everyone is entitled to his or her own understanding. No one group of people, including the clergy, has the exclusive right to interpret or reinterpret tenets of the faith. Some understandings may be more learned than others, but no version is automatically more authoritative than another.

A Religion That Can Grow

Islam is also a religion that can still grow, Soroush argues. It should not be used as a modern ideology, for it is too likely to become totalitarian. Yet he believes in shari'a, or Islamic law, as a basis for modern legislation. And shari'a, too, can grow. "Shari'a is something expandable. You cannot imagine the extent of its flexibility," he has said, adding that "in an Islamic democracy, you can actualize all its potential flexibilities."

The next broad subject that Soroush addresses is the clergy. The rights of the clergy are no greater than the privileges of anyone else, he argues. Thus in the ideal Islamic democracy, the clergy also have no a priori right to rule. The state should be run by whoever is popularly elected on the basis of equal rights under law.

Soroush advocates an even more fundamental change in the relationship between religion and both the people and the state. Religious leaders have traditionally received financial support from either the state (in most Sunni countries) or the people (in Shi'ite communities). In both cases, Soroush argues, the clergy should be "freed" so that they are not "captives" forced to propagate official or popular views rather than the faith of the Koran.

A religious calling is only for authentic lovers of religion and those who will work for it, Soroush says. No one should be able to be guaranteed a living, gain social status, or claim political power on the basis of religion. Clerics should work like everyone else, he says, making independent incomes through scholarship, teaching, or other jobs. Only such independence can prevent them—and Islam—from becoming compromised.

Finally, Soroush deals with the subject of secularism. Arabic, the language of Islam, does not have a literal translation for this word. But the nineteenth-century Arabic word *el-maniyya*—meaning "that which is rational or scientific"—comes close. In this context, Soroush views secularism not as the enemy or rival of religion, but as its complement: "It means to look at things scientifically and behave scientifically—which has nothing to do with hostility to religion. Secularism is nothing more than that." . . .

Rachid al-Ghannouchi

While Soroush prefers the cosmic overview, Rachid al-Ghannouchi's thinking is rooted in his experiences in Tunisia, and then applied to other Muslim societies. He has also been heavily influenced by Third World nationalism and the views of intellectuals from the global South who see their region as locked in a struggle against Northern "neo-colonialism." A popular philosophy teacher and speaker educated in Damascus and Paris, Ghannouchi founded the Mouvement de la Tendance Islamique (MTI) in 1981 during a brief interlude of Tunisian political liberalization. Tunisia's government refused to legalize the MTI, however, citing laws that excluded religious parties from politics. Ghannouchi persisted in calls on the regime to share power by introducing political pluralism and economic justice. He was jailed from 1981 to 1984; after his release, the authorities forbade him to teach, speak in public, publish, or travel.

In 1987, Ghannouchi was again arrested and charged with plotting to overthrow the government. He was released after a bloodless coup in November 1987, which led to another brief political thaw. The MTI, renamed al-Nahda in early 1989 to remove religious overtones, was promised a place at the political table. But by the time of the April 1989 legislative elections, the thaw was over. Reforms were stalled and confrontations mounted. Ghannouchi went into voluntary exile. The government charged al-Nahda with plotting a coup; the party was outlawed and Ghannouchi was sentenced in absentia to life imprisonment. Britain granted him political asylum in 1993, and he is now the most prominent Islamist leader living in the West. . . .

Ghannouchi advocates an Islamic system that features majority rule, free elections, a free press, protection of minorities, equality of all secular and religious parties, and full women's rights in everything from polling booths, dress codes, and divorce courts to the top job at the presidential palace. Islam's role is to provide the system with moral values.

Islamic democracy is first the product of scriptural interpretation. "Islam did not come with a specific program concerning our life," Ghannouchi said in one of several interviews between 1990 and 1995. "It brought general principles. It is our duty to formulate this program through interaction between Islamic principles and modernity." Believers are guaranteed the right of *ijtihad* in interpreting the Koranic text. Their empowerment is complete since Islam does not have an institution or person as a sole authority to represent the faith—or contradict their interpretations. The process of shura, moreover, means that decision making belongs to the community as a whole. "The democratic values of political pluralism and tolerance are perfectly compatible with Islam," he maintains.

Second, Islamic democracy is also a product of recent human experience. The legitimacy of contemporary Muslim states is based on liberation from modern European colonialism, a liberation in which religious and secular, Muslim and Christian, participated together. "There is no room to make distinctions between citizens, and complete equality is the base of any new Muslim society. The only legitimacy is the legitimacy of elections," he said. "Freedom comes before Islam and is the step leading to Islam."

Ghannouchi concedes that Islam's record in the areas of equality and participation has blemishes. Previous Muslim societies were built on conquest. But he contends that the faith has also traditionally recognized pluralism internally, noting the lack of religious wars among Muslims as proof of Islam's accommodation of the Muslim world's wide diversity. Citing the Koran, he explains that Islam condemns the use of religion for material or hegemonic purposes: "O mankind! We created you from a single [pair] of a male and a female, and made you into nations and tribes, that ye may know each other, not that ye may despise [each other]" (Sura 49:13).

Ghannouchi calls the act of striking a balance between holy texts and human reality *aqlanah*, which translates as "realism" or "logical reasoning." Aqlanah is dynamic and constantly evolving. As a result Ghannouchi, like Soroush, believes that Islam and democracy are an inevitable mix. In a wide-ranging address given in May 1995 at the Royal Institute of International Affairs in London, he said: "Once the Islamists are given a chance to comprehend the values of Western modernity, such as democracy and human rights, they will search within Islam for a place for these values where they will implant them, nurse them, and cherish them just as the Westerners did before, when they implanted such values in a much less fertile soil." He pledged al-Nahda's adherence to democracy and the alternation of power through the ballot box, and called on all other Islamist movements to follow suit in unequivocal language and even in formal pacts signed with other parties. . . .

A Long Way to Go

Christianity's Reformation took at least two centuries to work itself out. The Islamic Reformation is probably only somewhere in early midcourse. And the two movements offer only the roughest of parallels. The Christian Reformation, for example, was launched in reaction to the papacy and specific practices of the Catholic Church. In contrast, Islam has no central authority; even the chief ayatollah in the Islamic Republic of Iran is the supreme religious authority in one country only.

But the motives and goals of both reformations are similar. The Islamic reformers want to strip the faith of corrupt, irrelevant, or unjust practices that have been tacked on over the centuries. They are looking to make the faith relevant to changing times and conditions. They want to make the faith more accessible to the faithful, so that believers utilize the faith rather than have it used against them. And they want to draw on Islam as both a justification and a tool for political, social, and economic empowerment.

The Islamic reformist movement has a very long way to go. Although there are a handful of others besides Soroush and Ghannouchi making serious or original contributions to the debate, they still represent a distinct minority. The changes that they seek to promote will experience bumps, false starts, and failures, and may take a long time. Yet the Islamic Reformation represents the best hope for reconciliation both within Islam and between Islam and the outside world.

"*A basic premise of [Islamic law] is that no one, and especially no non-Muslim, may openly discuss certain subjects.*"

Islam Suppresses Freedom of Speech

Daniel Pipes

Daniel Pipes, director of the Middle East Forum and the author of several articles about Islam, alleges in the following viewpoint that fundamentalist Muslims attempt to stifle criticism of Islam through violence, threats, and mental intimidation. Furthermore, Pipes claims, some Islamic groups within the United States are working to suppress the freedoms of speech protected by the Constitution. If their attempts are successful, criticizing Islam may become a hate crime, he contends.

As you read, consider the following questions:
1. How have Muslims used physical intimidation to silence critics of Islam, according to Pipes?
2. What evidence does Pipes offer that American Islamists are attempting to curtail First Amendment freedoms?
3. What is the real agenda of the Council on American-Islamic Relations (CAIR), in the author's opinion?

Excerpted from Daniel Pipes, "'How Dare You Defame Islam,'" *Commentary*, November 1999. Reprinted with permission; all rights reserved.

The problem began in January 1989. That was when Muslims living in Bradford, England, decided to do something to show their anger about *The Satanic Verses,* a new novel by the famed writer Salman Rushdie that included passages making fun of the Prophet Muhammad. The Muslims, mostly Pakistani immigrants, purchased a copy of the novel, took it to a public square, attached it to a stake, and set it on fire. Television news showed this auto da fé in scandalized detail, and pictures of the scene were splashed across the British media for days, making it a major topic of discussion throughout the country.

In Pakistan itself, after a month's buildup, an unruly mob of some 10,000 anti-Rushdie protesters took to the streets of the capital city of Islamabad. Marching to the American Cultural Center (a fact significant in itself), they attempted with great energy, but without success, to set the heavily fortified building on fire. Six people died in the violence, and many more were injured.

These events, in turn, caught the attention of Ayatollah Khomeini, the revolutionary ruler of Iran, who took prompt and drastic action: on February 14, 1989, he called upon "all zealous Muslims quickly to execute" not just Salman Rushdie as the author of *The Satanic Verses* but "all those involved in its publication who were aware of its content." This edict led to emergency measures in England to protect Rushdie's person, and to weeks and months of intense debate among the world's politicians and intellectuals about the issues of freedom of speech and blasphemy.

When the dust settled, Khomeini had failed in his specific goal of eliminating Rushdie physically: today, over a decade later, the author is once again writing well-received books and accepting literary awards. But if Khomeini did not manage to harm Rushdie, he did accomplish something far more profound: he stirred the souls of many Muslims, reviving a sense of confidence in their faith and a strong impatience with any denigration of it, as well as a determination to take the offensive against anyone perceived to be a blasphemer or even a critic. Although Khomeini himself passed from the scene just weeks after issuing his decree, the spirit it engendered is very much alive.

Silencing Critics

During the decade since 1989, many efforts have been undertaken by the forces of Islamism—otherwise known as Muslim fundamentalism—to silence critics. Ranging from outright violence to more sophisticated but no less effective techniques, they have produced impressive results.

Some early acts of physical intimidation involved the Rushdie case itself. Translators of *The Satanic Verses* were stabbed and seriously injured in Norway and Italy and, in Japan, murdered. In Turkey, another translator escaped when a fire set in his hotel failed to kill him, but 37 others died in the blaze. Other acts of violence were designed to punish both Muslims and non-Muslims for a variety of alleged offenses.

Egypt alone offers a number of examples. Nasr Hamid Abu Zayd, a professor of literature who wrote that certain references in the Qur'an to supernatural phenomena should be read as metaphors, found his marriage dissolved by an Egyptian court on the grounds that his writings proved him an apostate. (According to Islamic law, a Muslim woman may not be married to a non-Muslim.) Another case involved the author of a nonconformist essay on Islam: he, his publisher, and the book's printer were each sentenced to eight years in jail on the charge of blasphemy. Farag Foda, an Egyptian intellectual who expressed scorn for the Islamist program, was shot and murdered. And Naguib Mahfouz, the elderly and much-celebrated Nobel Prize laureate for literature, was seriously injured in Cairo when an assailant knifed him in the neck, presumably in revenge for an allegorical novel written decades earlier.

Nor has the campaign been limited to Muslim-majority countries. Makin Morcos, also an Egyptian, was killed in Australia for criticizing the Islamists' anti-Christian campaign in his native country; Rashad Khalifa, a biochemist from Egypt living in Tucson, Arizona, was stabbed to death in January 1990 to silence his heretical ideas. (A member of Osama bin Laden's gang has been implicated in the latter murder.) Both these incidents sent a chilling message: you can run but you cannot hide.

Nor, finally, is the campaign in Western countries limited

to violence or threats of violence against Muslims; it also extends to non-Muslims. In some cases, purely private matters may be at issue: Jack Briggs, an Englishman, has been on the lam for years, hiding with his wife from her Pakistani family who have vowed to kill both of them (even though they are properly married and even though he converted to Islam to win their approval). Other cases concern publicly expressed views: Steven Emerson, a former Senate aide and investigative reporter for *U.S. News & World Report*, CNN, and other media, received death threats for *Jihad in America*, his award-winning television documentary that drew on the Islamists' own commercial videos to demonstrate their virulently anti-Semitic and anti-American views and activities.

Emerson told his story to a congressional committee in 1998, and it bears quoting at length:

> Immediately following the release of *Jihad in America*, I became the target of radical fundamentalist groups throughout the United States (and internationally) who fiercely denied the existence of "Islamic extremism" and accused me of engaging in an "attack against Islam." For this "transgression," my life has been permanently changed.

> Explaining the details of just one incident—to pick among a whole series—will help you understand the changes I have been forced to endure. One morning, in late 1995, I was paged by a federal law-enforcement official. When I returned the call, this official immediately instructed me to head downtown to his office and specifically directed me to take a taxi rather than my car. The urgency in this person's voice was palpable. When I arrived at the office, I was ushered into a room where a group of other law-enforcement officials were waiting. Within minutes, I found out why I had been summoned: I was told a group of radical Islamic fundamentalists had been assigned to carry out an assassination of me. An actual hit team had been dispatched from another country to the United States. The squad, according to the available intelligence, was to rendezvous with its American-based colleagues located in several U.S. cities. Compounding the jolt of being told about this threat was an additional piece of information: the assassination squad had been successfully able to elude law-enforcement surveillance.

> I was told that I had limited choices: since I was not a full-time government employee, I was not entitled to 24-hour-a-day police protection. However, I could probably get per-

mission to enter the Witness Security Program under the right circumstances. But the prospect of being spirited away and given a new identity was not acceptable to me—especially since that would afford the terrorists a moral victory in having shut me down. Frankly, however, the alternative option was not that attractive either—being on my own and taking my own chances. And yet that for me was the only effective option.

While Emerson remains doggedly on the trail of Islamists, especially those among them who support terrorism, he has for four years been forced to live at a clandestine address, always watching his movements. Like the case of Rashad Khalifa, murdered in Tucson for his views, the case of Steven Emerson suggests that, despite the Constitution's guarantees of freedom of religion and freedom of speech, when it comes to Islam, unapproved thinking can lead to personal danger or even death.

Forces of Intellectual Intimidation

Still, were force the only weapon in the Islamists' arsenal, their accomplishments would be limited. In the West, at least, violence and physical intimidation can achieve only so much. But, contrary to stereotype, Islamists are hardly all wild-eyed hit men and suicide bombers; in Western countries, many of them are quite at home with computers, well-versed in the latest lobbying techniques, and adept at the game of victimology. Energetic, determined, and skilled, they employ the tools not of physical but rather of intellectual intimidation. Their aim in doing so is to build an inviolate wall around Islam, endowing it with something like the sacrosanct status it enjoys in traditionally Muslim countries.

Islamists of this latter stripe make full use of every recourse available to them in the laws and customs of the Western liberal democracies themselves. A few examples will illustrate. In France, Marcel Lefebvre, a renegade Catholic bishop, was fined nearly $1,000 under French law for declaring that when the Muslim presence in France becomes stronger, "it is your wives, your daughters, your children who will be kidnapped and dragged off to a certain kind of place as they exist in [Morocco]." In Canada, a Christian activist handing out leaflets protesting the Muslim persecution of Christians was accused by Muslim organizations of "inciting hatred," found guilty of breaking Canada's hate-speech laws, and sentenced to 240 hours of community service and six months of probation time in jail. At the United Nations, the decidedly nondiplomatic epithets "blasphemy" and "defamation of Islam" have become part of normal discourse, serving as convenient instruments for shutting off discussion of such unpleasant matters as slavery in Sudan or Muslim anti-Semitism.

In the United States, where the concept of freedom of speech is sturdier than elsewhere, the First Amendment still

"I certainly hope we don't end up offending Islam."

prevents the government itself from fining or jailing anyone for offensive speech. But, relying on the ethos of political correctness that has resulted in such abridgements of First Amendment freedoms as university speech codes and other restrictive practices, Islamists seek to win what sanction they can to censor others. Thus, they have recently sponsored an innocent-sounding Senate resolution entitled "Supporting Religious Tolerance Toward Muslims." This resolution states as a fact that "Muslims have been subjected, simply because of their faith, to acts of discrimination and harassment that all too often have led to hate-inspired violence," and concludes that criticism of Islam, though legal in the strict sense, is morally reprehensible ("the Senate acknowledges that individuals and organizations that foster such intolerance create an atmosphere of hatred and fear that divides the Nation"). Should this resolution pass, and there is every reason to expect that it will, anyone with anything negative to say about Islam or Islamism can expect to be accused of fostering a hate crime.

Who, in the American context, is behind this campaign of mental intimidation and of what, in a journalistic context, would be called prior restraint? Among the many candidates, the leading one is surely the Council on American-Islamic Relations (CAIR), a Washington-based institution founded in 1994. CAIR presents itself to the world as a standard-issue civil-rights organization, whose mission is to "promote interest and understanding among the general public with regard to Islam and Muslims in North America and conduct educational services."

CAIR's Real Agenda

Sometimes, indeed, this is what CAIR does. In 1997, for example, it protested when an official at a meeting of a board of education in South Carolina said, "Screw the Buddhists and kill the Muslims." At other times, it has come to the defense of women who have lost their jobs for insisting on wearing a headscarf, or of men for wearing beards. But these occasional good works serve mostly as a cover for CAIR's real agenda, which appears to be twofold: to help the radical organization Hamas in its terror campaign against Israel, and to promote the Islamist program in the United States.

In furtherance of the first goal, CAIR regularly sends out "action alerts" to instigate dozens or even hundreds of protests, many of them vulgar and aggressive, whenever anyone dares to suggest publicly that Hamas or other terrorist networks operate in the United States, or indeed dares to support those who say such things. When Jeff Jacoby, a columnist for the *Boston Globe*, protested CAIR's almost successful effort to have Steven Emerson blacklisted from National Public Radio, CAIR cranked up its letter-writing campaign ("Dear JEW," went a characteristic missive from a CAIR minion, "How dare you defame Islam. . . . There is enough Muslim-bashing going on, I am sure your resigning will not make a difference to our jewish [sic] media") and, in a bit of raw intimidation, threatened the *Globe* with legal action. . . .

I do not want to leave the impression that CAIR represents the only opinion to be found in the Muslim community, either here or abroad. Shaykh Abdad Hadi Palazzi, for instance, secretary general of the Italian Muslim Association and director of the Cultural Institute of the Italian Muslim Community in Rome, has actually denounced CAIR for falsely claiming to represent the entire Muslim community while in reality being bent on launching "hate campaigns against journalists, Congressmen, Senators, and Muslims who interfere with [its] true terrorist agenda." What is more, Shaykh Palazzi has commended both me and Steven Emerson for daring to challenge the Islamists; though he does "not agree with [our] attitude toward Islam in particular and with [our] secular worldview in general," nevertheless we are to be lauded for distinguishing "authentic Islam from the counterfeit image presented by the Islamists"—of whom, the Shaykh pointedly concludes, Muslims themselves "are the main victims."

But Shaykh Palazzi is one among only a few voices of reason and sanity. Within the universe of Muslims who speak and write about Islam and its position in the modern world, the Islamists by far have the upper hand. That is not only a great tragedy for Muslims, but a danger to the rest of us. For if the Islamists have their way, any possibility of speaking the truth not only about them but about Islam itself will be foreclosed. Indeed, to a certain extent, as in the near-successful blacklisting of Steven Emerson at National Public Radio, it already has been.

Bernard Lewis, the renowned scholar of Islam and the Middle East, has noted with asperity that whereas, in this Christian country, an English-language biographer of Jesus enjoys total latitude to say what he will and as he will, his counterpart working on a biography of Muhammad must look fearfully over his shoulder every step of the way. About my own writing, one correspondent protested to the *National Post:* "It's interesting to me as a Muslim American to hear you, a non-Muslim, speak about Islam as an expert without you first consulting with an American Muslim organization like CAIR for an example, to get their opinion about what you are about to print." In other words, one is perfectly free to voice an opinion about Islam, provided that one has vetted its contents beforehand with the Islamists—roughly the situation that now prevails in Iran.

What the Islamists are demanding, in short, is that the United States take a giant step toward applying within its borders the strictures of Islamic law (the *shari'a*) itself. A basic premise of that body of law is that no one, and especially no non-Muslim, may openly discuss certain subjects—some of the very subjects, as it happens, that CAIR wishes to render taboo. However absurd this may seem to a casual observer—Muslims, after all, make up, at most, 2 percent of the U.S. population—it is a fact that, when the guard of the democratic majority is let down, determined minorities in pursuit of anti-democratic aims can sometimes get their way.

6

"Censorship is just as much a fact of life in Western societies as in the Muslim world."

Claims That Islam Suppresses Freedom of Speech Are Hypocritical

Ali A. Mazrui

The belief that Western societies are more "enlightened" than Muslim societies is hypocritical, argues Ali A. Mazrui in the following viewpoint. Islam and the West both curtail freedom of speech to some extent, he contends; the United States and other Western countries are simply more subtle about their methods of censorship. Mazrui is the director of the Institute of Global Cultural Studies at the State University of New York at Binghamton; Ibn Khaldun Professor-at-Large at the School of Islamic and Social Sciences in Leesburg, Virginia; and Senior Scholar in Africana Studies at Cornell University. He is also the author of several books, including *Cultural Forces in World Politics* and *The Power of Babel: Language and Governance in Africa's Experience.*

As you read, consider the following questions:

1. How does Mazrui challenge the notion that Western societies are significantly more enlightened than Islamic societies when it comes to the treatment of women?
2. According to the author, why was the novel *The Satanic Verses* by Salman Rushdie banned in some places?
3. Who are the practitioners of censorship in the West, in Mazrui's opinion?

Excerpted from Ali A. Mazrui, "Islamic and Western Values," *Foreign Affairs*, September/October 1997. Reprinted by permission of *Foreign Affairs*. Copyright 1997 by the Council on Foreign Relations, Inc.

Westerners tend to think of Islamic societies as backward-looking, oppressed by religion, and inhumanely governed, comparing them to their own enlightened, secular democracies. But measurement of the cultural distance between the West and Islam is a complex undertaking, and that distance is narrower than they assume. Islam is not just a religion, and certainly not just a fundamentalist political movement. It is a civilization, and a way of life that varies from one Muslim country to another but is animated by a common spirit far more humane than most Westerners realize. Nor do those in the West always recognize how their own societies have failed to live up to their liberal mythology. Moreover, aspects of Islamic culture that Westerners regard as medieval may have prevailed in their own culture until fairly recently; in many cases, Islamic societies may be only a few decades behind socially and technologically advanced Western ones. In the end, the question is what path leads to the highest quality of life for the average citizen, while avoiding the worst abuses. The path of the West does not provide all the answers; Islamic values deserve serious consideration.

The Way It Recently Was

Mores and values have changed rapidly in the West in the last several decades as revolutions in technology and society progressed. Islamic countries, which are now experiencing many of the same changes, may well follow suit. Premarital sex, for example, was strongly disapproved of in the West until after World War II. There were laws against sex outside marriage, some of which are still on the books, if rarely enforced. Today sex before marriage, with parental consent, is common.

Homosexual acts between males were a crime in Great Britain until the 1960s (although lesbianism was not outlawed). Now such acts between consenting adults, male or female, are legal in much of the West, although they remain illegal in most other countries. Half the Western world, in fact, would say that laws against homosexual sex are a violation of gays' and lesbians' human rights.

Even within the West, one sees cultural lag. Although capital punishment has been abolished almost everywhere in the Western world, the United States is currently increasing the number of capital offenses and executing more death row inmates than it has in years. But death penalty opponents, including Human Rights Watch and the Roman Catholic Church, continue to protest the practice in the United States, and one day capital punishment will almost certainly be regarded in America as a violation of human rights.

Westerners regard Muslim societies as unenlightened when it comes to the status of women, and it is true that the gender question is still troublesome in Muslim countries. Islamic rules on sexual modesty have often resulted in excessive segregation of the sexes in public places, sometimes bringing about the marginalization of women in public affairs more generally. British women, however, were granted the right to own property independent of their husbands only in 1870, while Muslim women have always had that right. Indeed, Islam is the only world religion founded by a businessman in commercial partnership with his wife. While in many Western cultures daughters could not inherit anything if there were sons in the family, Islamic law has always allocated shares from every inheritance to both daughters and sons. Primogeniture has been illegal under the sharia for 14 centuries.

The historical distance between the West and Islam in the treatment of women may be a matter of decades rather than centuries. Recall that in almost all Western countries except for New Zealand, women did not gain the right to vote until the twentieth century. Great Britain extended the vote to women in two stages, in 1918 and 1928, and the United States enfranchised them by constitutional amendment in 1920. France followed as recently as 1944. Switzerland did not permit women to vote in national elections until 1971—decades after Muslim women in Afghanistan, Iran, Iraq, and Pakistan had been casting ballots.

Furthermore, the United States, the largest and most influential Western nation, has never had a female president. In contrast, two of the most populous Muslim countries, Pakistan and Bangladesh, have had women prime ministers: Benazir Bhutto headed two governments in Pakistan, and Khaleda Zia and Hasina Wajed served consecutively in Bangladesh. Turkey has had Prime Minister Tansu Ciller. Muslim countries are ahead in female empowerment, though still behind in female liberation.

Concepts of the Sacred

Censorship is one issue on which the cultural divide between the West and Islam turns out to be less wide than Westerners ordinarily assume. The most celebrated case of the last decade—that of Salman Rushdie's novel *The Satanic Verses*, published in Britain in 1988 but banned in most Muslim countries—brought the Western world and the Muslim world in conflict, but also uncovered some surprising similarities and large helpings of Western hypocrisy. Further scrutiny reveals widespread censorship in the West, if imposed by different forces than in Muslim societies.

As their civilization has become more secular, Westerners have looked for new abodes of the sacred. By the late twentieth century the freedom of the artist—in this case, Salman Rushdie—was more sacred to them than religion. But many Muslims saw Rushdie's novel as holding Islam up to ridicule. The novel suggests that Islam's holy scripture, the Koran, is filled with inventions of the Prophet Muhammad or is, in fact, the work of the devil rather than communications from Allah, and implies, moreover, that the religion's founder was not very intelligent. Rushdie also puts women characters bearing the names of the Prophet's wives in a whorehouse, where the clients find the blasphemy arousing.

Many devout Muslims felt that Rushdie had no right to poke fun at and twist into obscenity some of the most sacred symbols of Islam. Most Muslim countries banned the novel because officials there considered it morally repugnant. Western intellectuals argued that as an artist, Rushdie had the sacred right and even duty to go wherever his imagination led him in his writing. Yet until the 1960s *Lady Chatterley's Lover* [a novel by D.H. Lawrence] was regarded as morally repugnant under British law for daring to depict an affair between a married member of the gentry and a worker on the estate. For a long time after Oscar Wilde's conviction for homosexual acts, *The Picture of Dorian Gray* was regarded as morally repugnant. Today other gay writers are up against a wall of prejudice.

The Satanic Verses was banned in some places because of fears that it would cause riots. Indian officials explained that they were banning the novel because it would inflame religious passions in the country, already aroused by Kashmiri separatism. The United States has a legal standard for preventive action when negative consequences are feared—"clear and present danger." But the West was less than sympathetic to India's warnings that the book was inflammatory. Rushdie's London publisher, Jonathan Cape, went ahead, and the book's publication even in far-off Britain resulted in civil disturbances in Bombay, Islamabad, and Karachi in which some 15 people were killed and dozens more injured.

Censorship of Muslims in America

According to [a] student at Washtenaw [Community College in Ann Arbor, Michigan], she was prevented from saying "in the name of God, most Merciful, most Gracious" at the beginning of one of her class presentations. Before the student could begin that presentation, the instructor handed her a letter stating that she could not utter the phrase as she had on a previous occasion.

The instructor's letter stated that the phrase was "inappropriate and unacceptable in an American classroom" and that the student must adapt to the "cultural expectations of the United States" and to the "American classroom." The letter also said that the instructor would interrupt the student and ask her to sit down if she attempted to utter the phrase. . . .

In a letter to Washtenaw President Larry L. Whitworth, CAIR [Council on American-Islamic Relations] wrote: "As you may know, this phrase is said many times each day whenever a Muslim begins any endeavor. It is entirely appropriate that [the student] repeat the phrase as a form of constitutionally-protected religious expression before beginning her presentation . . . we regard this incident as a gross violation of [the student's] basic right to freedom of speech and freedom of religious expression."

CAIR Action Alert, January 4, 2000. Available from http://www.cair-net.org/alerts/00/alert-226.html.

Distinguished Western publishers, however, have been known to reject a manuscript because of fears for the safety of their own. In 1996, Cambridge University Press turned down *Fields of Wheat, Rivers of Blood* by Anastasia Karakasi-dou, a sociological study on ethnicity in the Greek province of Macedonia, publicly acknowledging that it did so because of worries about the safety of its employees in Greece. If Jonathan Cape had cared as much about South Asian lives as it said it cared about freedom of expression, or as Cambridge University Press cared about its staff members in Greece, less blood would have been spilled.

Targets, sources, and methods of censorship differ, but censorship is just as much a fact of life in Western societies as in the Muslim world. Censorship in the latter is often crude, imposed by governments, *mullahs* and *imams*, and, more recently, militant Islamic movements. Censorship in the West, on the other hand, is more polished and decentralized. Its practitioners are financial backers of cultural activity and entertainment, advertisers who buy time on commercial television, subscribers of the Public Broadcasting System (PBS), influential interest groups including ethnic pressure groups, and editors, publishers, and other controllers of the means of communication. In Europe, governments, too, sometimes get into the business of censorship.

Censoring America

The threat to free speech in the United States comes not from the law and the Constitution but from outside the government. PBS, legally invulnerable on the issue of free speech, capitulated to other forces when faced with the metaphorical description in my 1986 television series "The Africans" of Karl Marx as "the last of the great Jewish prophets." The British version had included the phrase, but the American producing station, WETA, a PBS affiliate in Washington, deleted it without authorial permission so as not to risk offending Jewish Americans.

On one issue of censorship WETA did consult me. Station officials were unhappy I had not injected more negativity into the series' three-minute segment on Libya's leader, Muammar Qaddafi. First they asked for extra commentary on allegations that Libya sponsored terrorism. When I refused, they suggested changing the pictures instead—deleting one sequence that humanized Qaddafi by showing him visiting a hospital and substituting a shot of the Rome airport after a terrorist bombing. After much debate I managed to save the hospital scene but surrendered on the Rome airport addition, on condition that neither I nor the written caption implied that Libya was responsible for the bombing. But, ideally, WETA would have preferred to cut the whole segment.

WETA in those days had more in common with the censors in Libya than either side realized. Although the Libyans broadcast an Arabic version and seemed pleased with the series as a whole, they cut the Qaddafi sequence. The segment also offended Lynne Cheney, chair of the National Endowment for the Humanities, who demanded that the endowment's name be removed from the series credits. After she stepped down from her post, she called for the NEH to be abolished, citing "The Africans" as an example of the objectionable liberal projects that, she said, the endowment had tended to fund.

In another case of decentralized censorship that affected my own work, Westview Press in Boulder, Colorado, was about to go to press with my book *Cultural Forces in World Politics* when editors there announced they wanted to delete three chapters: one discussing *The Satanic Verses* as a case of cultural treason, another comparing the Palestinian intifada with Chinese students' 1989 rebellion in Tiananmen Square, and a third comparing the South African apartheid doctrine of separate homelands for blacks and whites with the Zionist doctrine of separate states for Jews and Arabs. Suspecting that I would have similar problems with most other major U.S. publishers, I decided that the book would be published exclusively by James Currey, my British publisher, and Heinemann Educational Books, the American offshoot of another British house, which brought it out in 1990. Not even universities in the United States, supposed bastions of intellectual freedom, have been free from censorship. Until recently the greatest danger to one's chances of getting tenure lay in espousing Marxism or criticizing Israel or Zionism.

The positive aspect of decentralized censorship in the West, at least with regard to books, is that what is unacceptable to one publisher may be acceptable to another; what is almost unpublishable in the United States may be easily publishable in Britain or the Netherlands. With national television, the choices are more restricted. Many points of view are banned from the screen, with the possibility of a hearing only on the public access stations with the weakest signals.

In Western societies as in Muslim ones, only a few points of view have access to the national broadcast media and publishing industry or even to university faculties. In both civilizations, certain points of view are excluded from the center and marginalized. The source of the censorship may be different, but censorship is the result in the West just as surely as in the Islamic world.

Periodical Bibliography

The following articles have been selected to supplement the diverse views presented in this chapter. Addresses are provided for periodicals not indexed in the *Readers' Guide to Periodical Literature*, the *Alternative Press Index*, the *Social Sciences Index*, or the *Index to Legal Periodicals and Books*.

Fouad Ajami	"Economic Reform and Islam Don't Have to Be Mutually Exclusive," *U.S. News & World Report*, July 28, 1997.
Louis Cantori	"Islam's Potential for Development," *World & I*, January 1997. Available from 3600 New York Ave. NE, Washington, DC 20002.
Economist	"Democracy and Islam," April 17, 1999. Available from 111 West 57th St., New York, NY 10019.
Dale F. Eickelman	"Inside the Islamic Reformation," *Wilson Quarterly*, Winter 1998.
Koenraad Elst	"The Rushdie Rules," *Middle East Quarterly*, June 1998. Available from PO Box 3000, Denville, NJ 07834.
John L. Esposito	"Islam & Christianity Face to Face," *Commonweal*, January 31, 1997.
Taslima Nasrin	"On Islamic Fundamentalism," *Humanist*, July/August 1996.
Daniel Pipes	"There Are No Moderates: Dealing with Fundamentalist Islam," *National Interest*, Fall 1995. Available from PO Box 622, Shrub Oak, NY 10588-0622.
David Pryce-Jones	"Twilight of the Ayatollahs," *National Review*, August 30, 1999.
I. Bruce Watson	"Islam and Its Challenges in the Modern World," *Insight*, May 1998.

CHAPTER 2

What Is the Status of Women Under Islam?

Chapter Preface

When Western societies discuss the status of women under Islam, the tradition of veiling frequently enters into the debate. Worn by most Muslim women throughout the world, the veil takes a variety of forms: The *hijab* covers only the hair; the black, cloaklike *chador* common in Iran conceals all but the face; the *niqab* veils the entire body and face except for a narrow opening that reveals the eyes; and the *burqa*, a required garment for women in Afghanistan, is all-encompassing, with only a small square of netting to allow for vision.

Westerners typically regard the veil as evidence that women are considered inferior by the Islamic faith. As Michele Lemon, a Canadian writer, explains, "How could anyone defend [the veil] as preserving anything but the low regard and true unimportance of women . . . ? . . . [A veiled] woman is a walking billboard that proclaims public space is reserved for men [and that] a woman's place is indoors."

However, many Muslim women resent the widespread belief that Muslim traditions of female dress are oppressive. In fact, according to Muslim feminists, the veil is a symbol of women's liberation because it allows women to be judged on their opinions instead of their physical appearance. Naheed Mustafa, a Muslim woman living in Canada, writes that "wearing the *hijab* has given me freedom from constant attention to my physical self. . . . Women are not going to achieve equality with the right to bear their breasts in public. . . . True equality will be had only when women don't need to display themselves to get attention."

The veil promises to be a source of further debate as Muslim women reinterpret its meaning. For example, wearing the Muslim headscarf has become a statement of rebellion in Turkey, whose secular government condemns displays of religious faith. The veil, and other issues relating to the status of women under Islam, are examined in further detail in the following chapter.

"The Qur'an does not discriminate on the basis of gender."

Islam Supports Gender Equality

Mahjabeen Islam-Husain

In the following viewpoint, Mahjabeen Islam-Husain contends that Islam promotes equality for women. According to Islam-Husain, the Qur'an, Islam's holy book, mandates that women have the right to seek education, choose their own mates, work, possess and inherit wealth or property, divorce, and remarry. Despite the Qur'an's clear support for women's rights, writes the author, many Muslim societies neglect to follow these teachings. Islam-Husain holds that the oppression of women within Muslim countries betrays Islam's principle of gender equality. Islam-Husain is a family practice physician and a Sunni Muslim. Born in Pakistan, she now lives in the midwestern United States and is active in the Muslim-American community.

As you read, consider the following questions:
1. According to Mahjabeen Islam-Husain, how does Islam provide financial security to women?
2. Why are Muslim women "the most oppressed in the world," as the author claims?
3. In Islam-Husain's view, what was the intention of polygamy, as conceived by the Qur'an?

Reprinted from Mahjabeen Islam-Husain, "It's Up to Muslim Women to Reclaim Our God-Given Rights," *Washington Report on Middle East Affairs*, June/July 1997, with permission.

Overall we get a pretty bad rap, don't you think? We Muslims, I mean. Fanatical suicide bombers in search of a little heaven. And Muslim women? How does the world view them? Repressed, enshrouded and mindless is a brusque yet probably accurate description. Should Muslims be offended by this impression? I wonder.

At the outset, however, a distinction must be made between what Islam teaches as opposed to what Muslims have made of Islam. This is the point that personally hurts me the most: that Muslims, especially in regards to the rights and duties of women, have made such a hash of the doctrine of our great faith.

Mankind, as the Qur'an says, "created in the best structure" (95:4), has been placed on Earth as Allah's *khalifa* or vice-regent (Qur'an 2:30). Fortunately for us Muslims, the Day of Reckoning will be primarily on an individual basis, as Islam is a deeds-based religion. On that Day our earthly sojourn will be recreated for us to view and understand the reward/punishment.

Thank goodness it will be primarily individual, for if it were not then as a collective whole Muslims through the ages would have a great deal of explaining to do for interpreting the Qur'an, the Hadith (sayings of the Prophet Muhammad), the Sunnah (life of the Prophet Muhammad), *shariah* (Divine Law, laid down in the Qur'an) and *fiqh* (jurisprudential issues) in a subjective manner skewed to one's own bias.

Nowhere does this apply as much as in the rights of women, where patriarchal Muslim societies have shortchanged women so much and for so long that the fallout has been exponential. The Qur'an does not discriminate on the basis of gender. "For Muslim men and women, for believing men and women, for devout men and women, for true men and women, for men and women who are patient and constant, for men and women who humble themselves, for men and women who give in charity, for men and women who fast, for men and women who guard their chastity, and for men and women who engage in Allah's praise—for them has Allah prepared forgiveness and a great reward" (Qur'an 33:35).

The Qur'an Does Not Discriminate on the Basis of Gender

Additionally, the Qur'an, recognizing the vulnerability of women and their great potential for exploitation, is very specific about women's rights, as illustrated by these examples:

1) Abolition of female infanticide: In pre-Islamic Arabia, killing female children was a widespread practice. This was completely forbidden by Islam. "When news is brought to one of them of [the birth of] a female [child], his face darkens and he is filled with inward grief! With shame he hides himself from his people because of the bad news he has had! Shall he retain her on contempt or bury her in the dust? Ah! What an evil [choice] they decide on!" (Qur'an 16:58-59).

It is reported that this barbaric practice continues today in India and China, where fetal ultrasounds are done and if it is a female fetus, some women undergo abortions. Having a son retains its "security," both financial and emotional, as it did in the days of *jahilliyah* or "ignorance" of pre-Islamic Arabia.

Muslims, on the other hand, must understand the concept of not relying on anyone but God alone. In fact, seeking security through sons, wealth, investments, or clout and influence, is akin to *shirk*, or equating any entity to God. This is a sin that Allah has said repeatedly in the Qur'an will never be forgiven.

2) Equal education opportunity: Islam equates attainment of knowledge to *ibadah*, or worship of Allah, recommending travel to China if need be to attain knowledge. Both sexes are dealt with equitably. "If any do deeds of righteousness, be they male or female, and have faith, they will enter Paradise and not the least injustice will be done to them" (Qur'an 4:124).

3) The right to choose her mate: A woman cannot be married against her will. The expression of her will should occur during the selection process, and not at the "I do" part. The majority of Muslim marriages are still arranged, and it is advisable that the woman be an integral part of the decision-making process from start to finish. The marriage is null and void if free consent is not given by both husband and wife.

4) The right to employment: Despite the male chauvinism of Muslim (actually all) societies, as well as the West's concept of the Muslim female as a cloistered, voiceless entity, Islam allows women to work outside the home. This is on condition that decency of attire is observed, the nurturing of the family is not compromised and the prior permission of the husband is obtained.

The rights of men and women in Islam therefore are not identical, but very equitable. There is not absolute mirror-image equality because of the difference in physical capabilities (pregnancy, nursing) and vulnerability, and the different role men and women play in society. Allah in His infinite wisdom has made it mandatory on the husband to be the provider for the family, so that with all the travails of child-bearing and rearing, a woman does not have to undergo the additional stress of bringing money home.

Safeguarding the Family

In Islam the family is the most important unit of society, and safeguarding the interests of all its members is paramount. Just as two CEOs are not hired in a corporation, in a Muslim family the husband and wife are to play complementary roles, deciding jointly about issues, though the onus of the final decision is on the husband. Perhaps this is why women are required to obtain the permission of the husband prior to employment.

Here, actually, is the problem. Muslim males have exercised this right on the basis of incorrect information transmitted by mullahs (religious leaders) who have reduced women to pathetic receptacles of procreation, all in the name of Islam. They even have gotten away with this coercion for several centuries because of the illiteracy of their female "subjects," who are caught in the vicious circle of ignorance and consequent inertia. The Qur'an in fact states that women are to be confined to their homes only as a punishment for lewdness (Qur'an 4:15). Seen in this light, it seems that Muslim societies have overdone things a little.

5) The right to her earnings, property and wealth: The Qur'an states "men shall have of what they earn and women shall have of what they earn" (4:32). If Islam cloistered women, the question of women keeping their earnings would not arise, as homemakers are not paid for their work and it is implicit that these "earnings" come from outside employment. This is a right of which many enlightened Muslim women take full advantage. Since the husband is to support the family, regardless of his financial status, a woman gets to keep her earnings, spending them on the family according to her discretion. In real life, obviously, a wife and mother would not deprive her family if she were able and the husband were not.

What the Qur'an Says About Women

In Islam there is absolutely no difference between men and women as far as their relationship to Allah is concerned, as both are promised the same reward for good conduct and the same punishment for evil conduct. The Qur'an says:

> *And for women are rights over men similar to those of men over women. (2:226)*

The Qur'an, in addressing the believers, often uses the expression, "believing men and women" to emphasize the equality of men and women in regard to their respective duties, rights, virtues and merits. It says:

> *For Muslim men and women, for believing men and women, for devout men and women, for true men and women, for men and women who are patient and constant, for men and women who humble themselves, for men and women who give in charity, for men and women who fast, for men and women who guard their chastity, and for men and women who engage much in Allah's praise, for them has Allah prepared forgiveness and great reward. (33:35) . . .*

The Qur'an admonishes those men who oppress or ill-treat women:

> *O you who believe! You are forbidden to inherit women against their will. Nor should you treat them with harshness, that you may take away part of the dowry you have given them—except when they have become guilty of open lewdness. On the contrary live with them on a footing of kindness and equity. If you take a dislike to them, it may be that you dislike something and Allah will bring about through it a great deal of good. (4:19)*

Abdur Rahman I. Doi, "Women in the Qur'an and the Sunna." Available at http://www.usc.edu/dept/MSA/humanrelations/womeninislam/womenquransunnah.html.

6) The right to inherit and financial security: Prior to the advent of Islam women were nonentities. Islam gave us the right to ownership and to inherit property. "From what is left by parents and those nearest related, there is a share for men and a share for women, whether the property be small or large—a determinate share" (Qur'an 4:7). Critics have argued about the lower share of the woman as compared to a man, disregarding the fact that a man has to provide for his mother, sister, daughter and all women related to him, whereas a woman again gets to keep her share.

Islam provides financial security to a woman by requiring a man to pay the woman *mahr* at the time of marriage. This gift may be foregone initially, but the woman reserves the right to collect unpaid *mahr* at the time of divorce. This is an amount that is mutually determined prior to marriage. A man also is obligated to support a woman during the *iddah* period after a divorce. This is the equivalent of three menstrual cycles or four months, and is provided to ensure the paternity of a possible pregnancy.

An Equal Right to Divorce and Remarry

7) The right to divorce: Unlike Catholicism, Orthodox Judaism and Hinduism, Islam does not condemn a woman to a lifetime of a failed, repressive, disillusioned or abusive relationship. In regards to divorce the Qur'an says, "In a fair manner women have the same rights against their men as men have against them" (2:228).

Pious men and women are advised to work out their differences, and divorce, though allowed, is abhorred by Islam. "And if you fear a breach between the couple, then send an arbitrator from his family and an arbitrator from her family; if they both desire compromise, God will effect harmony between the couple: verily God is All-Knowing, All-Aware" (Qur'an 4:35). In the event of cruelty, impotence, insanity or absolutely irreconcilable differences the woman can seek a divorce.

It's tragic indeed that with probably the most liberating religion, Muslim women are the most oppressed in the world. The reasons are multifactorial: patriarchal, male-dominated societies, illiteracy, poverty, the consequent dependence on men and the daily struggle for survival. All these preclude women understanding our God-given rights, let alone demanding them from society.

8) The right to remarry: In some other religions that do not allow divorce, the question of remarriage does not arise. A

Muslim woman, however, need not remain a stigmatized divorcee. She can remarry, although she is obligated to marry a Muslim. In the event of widowhood, also, a woman can remarry after finishing the required period of *iddah*.

The Issue of Polygamy

The very controversial and greatly abused concept of polygamy has served as the "Sword of Damocles" for Muslim women for ages. Islam did not outlaw polygamy, but regulated and restricted it. It is neither required nor encouraged, only permitted. Edward Westermarck, in *The History of Human Marriage*, gives numerous examples of polygamy among Jews, Christians and others. The only passage in the Qur'an (4:3) that explicitly addresses polygamy and restricts its practice in terms of the number of wives permitted, and the requirement of justice between them on the part of the husband, was revealed after the battle of Uhud, in which dozens of Muslims were martyred, leaving behind widows and orphans. "If you fear that you shall not be able to deal justly with the orphans, marry women of your choice, two or three or four: but if you fear that you shall not be able to deal justly with them, then only one . . ." (Qur'an 4:3). This seems to indicate that the reason for its continued permissibility is to deal with individual and collective contingencies that may arise. It provides a moral, practical and humane solution to the problems of widows and orphans who, in the absence of a father figure, would suffer in terms of economics, companionship, proper child rearing, etc. A woman, however, may specify in a prenuptial contract that the man will practice monogamy and, in the event of the man violating the contract, that his first wife will be entitled to seek divorce with all its associated financial rights.

Recognizing the difficulty in being totally fair to women, the Qur'an states, "You will never be able to attain justice between women [wives] even though you may covet it, so incline not with a total inclination to one so that you leave her as it were in suspense; and if you effect a reconciliation and guard yourself against evil, verily then God is oft oft-forgiving merciful" (4:129). Mullahs have interpreted this to mean that since men cannot be fair to women and since God is oft-forgiving

82

most merciful, the enforcement of Qur'anic teachings regarding justice to all wives is not required in a strict fashion. The fact that the Qur'an takes note of a human failing with a forbearing attitude is thus taken by many Muslims to be a justification for disregard of a clearly enunciated highly stressed injunction. Polygamy, as conceived by the Qur'an, was to be practiced for the benefit of women and children, and not as a means of satisfying male sensuality and wantonness.

Despite skewed interpretations of the Qur'an by Muslims, there are still situations where polygamy is an alternative which dependent, destitute, chronically ill or otherwise disadvantaged women prefer to divorce or abandonment by the husband.

As far as the enshrouded Muslim woman is concerned, there is a misconception in the West that a Muslim woman is forced to dress modestly by the male elite. Excluding the Taliban of Afghanistan, who are placing unreasonable demands on society in the name of Islam, a great number of Muslim women observe *hijab* due to their personal conviction regarding the recommendation of modest attire by Islam.

Unfortunately, no Muslim society is a paragon of Islam. The famous Pakistani poet Allama Iqbal said no community's state is changed by God except for the community that wants to change its situation. It is true that Muslim women are oppressed and underrepresented due to the male-dominated, economically backward societies they live in. Muslim women are, however, the only force that can break the ignorance-inertia-oppression cycle in which they are caught. In various Muslim countries there are movements toward this.

Interestingly, the one place where this is very practicable is the United States, because here putting belief into action is not a distant mirage. Again, only we Muslim women, through education, action and courage, can reclaim what in actuality are our God-given rights.

*"Islam has always considered women as
creatures inferior in every way: physically,
intellectually, and morally."*

Islam Supports Gender
Inequality

Ibn Warraq

Ibn Warraq, raised as a Muslim, criticizes Islamic beliefs and
practices in *Why I Am Not a Muslim*, from which the following viewpoint is excerpted. Warraq argues that Islam is
by definition a misogynous religion, since its holy scriptures
explicitly state that women are inferior to men and thus do
not deserve the same rights as men. The tenets of Islam are
used to justify the oppression of women in Muslim societies,
Warraq claims.

As you read, consider the following questions:
1. What is the woman's role, as defined by Muslim
   philosopher al-Ghazali?
2. In what ways are Muslim marriages unequal, according
   to Warraq?
3. As stated by the author, how do the *Zina* and *Hudud*
   Ordinances in Pakistan discriminate against women?

Excerpted from Ibn Warraq, "Islam's Shame: Lifting the Veil of Tears," *Free
Inquiry*, vol. 17, no. 4 (Fall 1997). Reprinted by permission of the Council for
Democratic and Secular Humanism.

I slam is deeply anti-woman. Islam is the fundamental cause of the repression of Muslim women and remains the major obstacle to the evolution of their position. Islam has always considered women as creatures inferior in every way: physically, intellectually, and morally. This negative vision is divinely sanctioned in the Koran, corroborated by the *hadiths* [traditions or sayings attributed to the prophet Muhammad], and perpetuated by the commentaries of the theologians, the custodians of Muslim dogma and ignorance. . . .

Profoundly Anti-Woman

The Islamic tradition . . . attributes guile and deceit to women and draws its support from the Koran. Modern Muslim commentators interpret certain verses to show that guile, deceit, and treachery are intrinsic to a woman's nature. Not only is she unwilling to change, she is by nature incapable of changing—she has no choice. In attacking the female deities of the polytheists, the Koran takes the opportunity to malign the female sex further.

4.1 17. They invoke in His stead only females; they pray to none else than Satan, a rebel.

53.21–22. Are yours the males and His the females? That indeed were an unfair division!

53.27. Lo! it is those who disbelieve in the Hereafter who name the angels with the names of females.

Other verses from the Koran also seem of a misogynist tendency.

2.228. Women who are divorced shall wait, keeping themselves apart, three (monthly) courses. And it is not lawful for them that they should conceal that which Allah hath created in their wombs if they are believers in Allah and the Last Day. And their husbands would do better to take them back in that case if they desire a reconciliation. And they (women) have rights similar to those (of men) over them in kindness, and men are a degree above them. Allah is Mighty, Wise.

2.282. But if he who oweth the debt is of low understanding, or weak or unable himself to dictate, then let the guardian of his interests dictate in (terms of) equity. And call to witness, from among your men, two witnesses. And if two men be not (at hand) then a man and two women, of such as ye approve as witnesses, so that if the one erreth (through forgetfulness) the other will remember.

4.11. Allah chargeth you concerning (the provision for) your children: to the male the equivalent of the portion of two females.

4.34. Men are in charge of women, because Allah hath made the one of them to excel the other, and because they spend of their property (for the support of women). So good women are the obedient, guarding in secret that which Allah hath guarded. As for those from whom ye fear rebellion, admonish them and banish them to beds apart; and scourge (beat) them. Then if they obey you, seek not a way against them. Lo! Allah is ever High Exalted, Great.

The Women's Role in Islam

Equally, in numerous *hadiths* on which are based the Islamic laws, we learn of the woman's role—to stay at home, to be at the beck and call of man to obey him (which is a religious duty), and to assure man a tranquil existence. Here are some examples of these traditions:

- The woman who dies and with whom the husband is satisfied will go to paradise.
- A wife should never refuse herself to her husband even if it is on the saddle of a camel.
- Hellfire appeared to me in a dream and I noticed that it was above all peopled with women who had been ungrateful. "Was it toward God that they were ungrateful?" They had not shown any gratitude toward their husbands for all they had received from them. Even when all your life you have showered a woman with your largesse she will still find something petty to reproach you with one day, saying, "You have never done anything for me."
- If anything presages a bad omen it is: a house, a woman, a horse.
- Never will a people know success if they confide their affairs to a woman.

It will be appropriate to include two quotes from the famous and much revered philosopher al-Ghazali (1058–1111), whom Professor Montgomery Watt describes as the greatest Muslim after Muhammad. In his "The Revival of the Religious Sciences," Ghazali defines the woman's role:

> She should stay at home and get on with her spinning, she should not go out often, she must not be well-informed, nor must she be communicative with her neighbours and only visit them when absolutely necessary; she should take care of her husband and respect him in his presence and his absence and seek to satisfy him in everything; she must not cheat on him nor extort money from him; she must not leave her house without his permission and if given his permission she must leave surreptitiously. She should put on old clothes and take deserted streets and alleys, avoid markets, and make sure that a stranger does not hear her voice or recognize her; she must not speak to a friend of her husband even in need. . . . Her sole worry should be her virtue, her home as well as her prayers and her fast. If a friend of her husband calls when the latter is absent she must not open the door nor reply to him in order to safeguard her and her husband's honour. She should accept what her husband gives her as sufficient sexual needs at any moment. . . . She should be clean and ready to satisfy her husband's sexual needs at any moment.

Such are some of the sayings from the putative golden age of Islamic feminism. It was claimed that it was the abandonment of the original teachings of Islam that had led to the present decadence and backwardness of Muslim societies. But there never was an Islamic utopia. To talk of a golden age is only to conform and perpetuate the influence of the clergy, the *mullas*, and their hateful creed that denies humanity to half the inhabitants of this globe, and further retards all serious attempts to liberate Muslim women.

What Rights?

The inequality between men and women in matters of giving testimony or evidence or being a witness is enshrined in the Koran: *sura* [chapter] 2.282 (quoted above).

How do Muslim apologists justify the above text? Muslim men and women writers point to the putative psychological differences that exist between men and women. The Koran (and hence God) in its sublime wisdom knew that women are sensitive, emotional, sentimental, easily moved, and influenced by their biological rhythm, lacking judgment. But above all they have a shaky memory. In other words, women are psychologically inferior. Such are the dubious arguments used by Muslim intellectuals—male and, astonishingly enough, female intellectuals like Ahmad Jamal, Ms. Zahya Kaddoura, Ms. Ghada al-Kharsa, and Ms. Madiha Khamis. As Ghassan Ascha points out, the absurdity of their arguments are obvious.

By taking the testimony of two beings whose reasoning faculties are faulty we do not obtain the testimony of one complete person with a perfectly functioning rational faculty—such is Islamic arithmetic! By this logic, if the testimony of two women is worth that of one man, then the testimony of four women must be worth that of two men, in which case we can dispense with the testimony of the men. But no! In Islam the rule is not to accept the testimony of women alone in matters to which men theoretically have access. It is said that the Prophet did not accept the testimony of women in matters of marriage, divorce, and *hudud*. *Hudud* are the punishments set down by Muhammad in the Koran and the *hadith* for (1) adultery—stoning to death; (2) fornication—a hundred stripes; (3) false accusation of adultery against a married person—eighty stripes; (4) apostasy—death; (5) drinking wine—eighty stripes; (6) theft—the cutting off of the right hand; (7) simple robbery on the highway—the loss of hands and feet; robbery with murder—death, either by the sword or by crucifixion. . . .

Unequal Testimony

In the case where a man suspects his wife of adultery or denies the legitimacy of the offspring, his testimony is worth that of four men. *Sura* 24.6: "If a man accuses his wife but has no witnesses except himself, he shall swear four times by God that his charge is true, calling down upon himself the curse of God if he is lying. But if his wife swears four times by God that his charge is false and calls down His curse upon herself if it be true, she shall receive no punishment." Appearances to the contrary, this is not an example of Koranic justice or equality between the sexes. The woman indeed escapes being stoned to death but she remains rejected and loses her right to the dowry and her right to maintenance, *whatever the outcome of the trial.* A woman does not have the right to charge her husband in a similar manner. Finally, for a Muslim marriage to be valid there must be a multiplicity of witnesses. For Muslim jurists, two men form a multiplicity but not two or three or a thousand women.

In questions of heritage, the Koran tells us that male children should inherit twice the portion of female children:

> 4.11–12. A male shall inherit twice as much as a female. If there be more than two girls, they shall have two-thirds of the inheritance, but if there be one only, she shall inherit the half. Parents shall inherit a sixth each, if the deceased have a child; but if he leave no child and his parents be his heirs, his mother shall have a third. If he have brothers, his mother shall have a sixth after payment of any legacy he may have bequeathed or any debt he may have owed.

To justify this inequality, Muslim authors lean heavily on the fact that a woman receives a dowry and has the right to maintenance from her husband. It is also true that according to Muslim law the mother is not at all obliged to provide for her children, and if she does spend money on her children, it is, to quote G.H. Bousquet, "recoverable by her from her husband if he is returned to a better fortune as in the case of any other charitable person. Therefore there is no point in the husband and wife sharing in the taking charge of the household; this weighs upon the husband alone. There is no longer any financial interest between them."

Inequalities in Muslim Marriage

This latter point referred to by Bousquet simply emphasizes the negative aspects of a Muslim marriage—that is to say, the total absence of any idea of "association" between "couples" as in Christianity. As to dowry, it is, of course, simply a reconfirmation of the man's claims over the woman in matters of sex and divorce. Furthermore, in reality the woman does not get to use the dowry for herself. The custom is either to use the dowry to furnish the house of the newly married couple or for the wife to offer it to her father. According to the Malekites, the woman can be obliged by law to use the dowry to furnish the house. Muslim law also gives the guardian the right to cancel a marriage—even that of a woman of legal age—if he thinks the dowry is not sufficient. Thus the dowry, instead of being a sign of her independence, turns out once more to be a symbol of her servitude.

The woman has the right to maintenance but this simply emphasizes her total dependence on her husband, with all its attendant sense of insecurity. According to Muslim jurists, the husband is not obliged under Islamic law to pay for her medical expenses in case of illness. Financial independence of the woman would of course be the first step in the liberation of Muslim women and thus it is not surprising that it is seen as a threat to male dominance. Muslim women are now obliged to take equal responsibility for looking after their parents. Article 158 of Syrian law states, "The child—male or female—having the necessary means is obliged to take responsibility for his or her poor parents." The birth of a girl is still seen as a catastrophe in Islamic societies. The system of inheritance just adds to her misery and her dependence on the man. If she is an only child she receives only half the legacy of her father; the other half goes to the male members of the father's family. If there are two or more daughters, they inherit two-thirds. This pushes fathers and mothers to prefer male children to female so that they can leave the entirety of their effects or possessions to their own descendants. "Yet when a new-born girl is announced to one of them his countenance darkens and he is filled with gloom" (*sura* 43.15). The situation is even worse when a woman loses her husband—she only receives a quarter of the legacy. If the deceased leaves more than one wife, all the wives are still obliged to share among themselves a quarter or one-eighth of the legacy. . . .

Case Histories: The Women of Pakistan

In Pakistan in 1977, General Zia al-Haq took over in a military coup declaring that the process of Islamization was not going fast enough. The *mullas* had finally got someone who was prepared to listen to them.

Zia imposed martial law, total press censorship, and began creating a theocratic state, believing that Pakistan ought to have "the spirit of Islam." He banned women from athletic contests and even enforced the Muslim fast during the month of Ramadan at gunpoint. He openly admitted that there was a contradiction between Islam and democracy. Zia introduced Islamic laws that discriminated against women.

The most notorious of these laws were the *Zina* and *Hudud* Ordinances that called for the Islamic punishments of the amputation of hands for stealing and stoning to death for married people found guilty of illicit sex. The term *zina* included adultery, fornication, and rape, and even prostitution. Fornication was punished with a maximum of a hundred lashes administered in public and ten years' imprisonment.

Muslim Women's Burdens

- Most Muslim countries embrace the teaching that women are lower than men because Eve was made from Adam's rib—and because Eve caused the Fall.

- In Pakistan, a woman may be denied a male partner by being "married off" to the Qur'an to prevent the division of land and deprive her of her inheritance.

- Husbands, but not wives, have the right of polygamy.

- In some countries, a woman's testimony in a court of law carries far less weight than a man's.

- In Saudi Arabia, women are not allowed to drive a car.

Ahmar Mustikhan and Massoud Ansari, *World & I*, February 1998.

In practice, these laws protect rapists, for a woman who has been raped often finds herself charged with adultery or fornication. To prove *zina*, four Muslim adult males of good repute must be present to testify that sexual penetration has taken place. Furthermore, in keeping with good Islamic practice, these laws value the testimony of men over women. The combined effect of these laws is that it is impossible for a woman to bring a successful charge of rape against a man; instead, she herself, the victim, finds herself charged with illicit sexual intercourse, while the rapist goes free. If the rape results in a pregnancy, this is automatically taken as an admission that adultery or fornication has taken place with the woman's consent rather than that rape has occurred.

Here are some sample cases.

Rape

In a town in the northern province of Punjab, a woman and her two daughters were stripped naked, beaten, and gang-raped in public, but the police declined to pursue the case.

A thirteen-year-old girl was kidnapped and raped by a "family friend." When her father brought a case against the rapist, it was the girl who was put in prison and charged with *zina*, illegal sexual intercourse. The father managed to secure the child's release by bribing the police. The traumatized child was then severely beaten for disgracing the family honor.

A fifty-year-old widow, Ahmedi Begum, decided to let some rooms in her house in the city of Lahore to two young veiled women. As she was about to show them the rooms, the police burst into the courtyard of the house and arrested the two girls and Ahmedi Begum's nephew, who had simply been standing there. Later that afternoon, Ahmedi Begum went to the police station with her son-in-law to inquire about her nephew and the two girls. The police told Ahmedi they were arresting her too. They confiscated her jewelry and pushed her into another room. While she was waiting, the police officers shoved the two girls, naked and bleeding, into the room and then proceeded to rape them again in front of the widow. When Ahmedi covered her eyes, the police forced her to watch by pulling her arms to her sides. After suffering various sexual humiliations, Ahmedi herself was stripped and raped by one officer after another. They dragged her outside where she was again beaten. One of the officers forced a policeman's truncheon, covered with chili paste, into her rectum, rupturing it. Ahmedi screamed in horrible agony and fainted, only to wake up in prison, charged with *zina*. Her case was taken up by a human rights lawyer. She was released on bail after three months in prison, but was not acquitted until three years later. In the meantime, her son-in-law divorced her daughter because of his shame.

Was this an isolated case? Unfortunately no. The Human Rights Commission of Pakistan said in its annual report that one woman is raped every three hours in Pakistan and one in two rape victims is a juvenile. According to Women's Action Forum, a woman's rights organization, 72% of all women in police custody in Pakistan are physically and sexually abused. Furthermore, 75% of all women in jail are there under charges of *zina*. Many of these women remain in jail awaiting trial for years.

In other words, the charge of *zina* is casually applied by any man who wants to get rid of his wife, who is immediately arrested, and kept waiting in prison, sometimes for years. Before the introduction of these laws the total number of women in prison was 70; the present number is more than 3,000. Most of these women have been charged under the *Zina* or *Hudud* Ordinances.

> "With the coming to power of Islamic fundamentalists in 1992, [Afghan] women's right to full participation in social, economic, cultural and political life . . . was drastically curtailed."

Islamic Fundamentalism in Afghanistan Oppresses Women

Revolutionary Association of the Women of Afghanistan

On September 27, 1996, an Islamic militia called the Taliban seized control of the government of Afghanistan. Among the Taliban's many new decrees were laws that prohibit women from working, obtaining an education, and even receiving medical care. The Revolutionary Association of the Women of Afghanistan contends that such injustices are the product of Islamic fundamentalism, which views women as subhuman. RAWA is an organization of Afghan women fighting for peace, freedom, democracy, and women's rights in Afghanistan.

As you read, consider the following questions:
1. How do the Islamic fundamentalists of Afghanistan treat women, as explained by the author?
2. What type of garment must Afghan women wear in public, according to RAWA?
3. Under the Taliban, what type of behavior warrants public beatings for women, as cited by RAWA?

Excerpted from the report "On the Situation of Afghan Women," on the website of the Revolutionary Association of the Women of Afghanistan, www.rawa.org. No date. Reprinted with permission.

Of the estimated 16 million Afghans at the end of the '70s, over two million have been killed in the war of resistance against Soviet occupiers and later on in the civil war unleashed by fundamentalist groupings enjoying the support of foreign powers. Another one and half million have been maimed by the war fallout, while nearly five million have been forced into refugee camps in Iran and Pakistan. The majority of the population left inside the country have been internally displaced as a result of the unending war of the past two decades and in particular of the fundamentalist infighting since 1992. At the best of times the overall literacy rate was less than 15% amongst males and less than 5% amongst females. (These figures are considered by some as very optimistic.) Against such a backdrop, the country slid into the hands of Islamic fundamentalists in 1992.

Women as Sub-Humans

Islamic fundamentalism in essence looks upon women as sub-humans, fit only for household slavery and as a means of procreation. Such an outrageous view has incredibly been elevated to the status of official policy with the coming to power of the ultra-fundamentalist Taliban who are still in control of two-thirds of Afghanistan including the capital Kabul. Not only the fundamentalists and ultra-fundamentalists but all Islamists (advocates of an Islamic political system) target women's rights as a first priority, citing medieval Sharia law as their authority. With the coming to power of Islamic fundamentalists in 1992, [Afghan] women's right to full participation in social, economic, cultural and political life . . . was drastically curtailed and later on summarily denied them by the ultra-fundamentalist Taliban. Under the latter, who are the predominant political power in Afghanistan today, women are totally deprived of the right to education (all girls' schools have been closed down), of the right to work (all women have been ordered to remain in their houses and employers have been threatened with dire consequences for taking up female employees), of the right to travel (no woman can venture out of the house alone and unaccompanied by a prescribed male member of the woman's immediate family), of the right to health (no woman can see a male doctor, fam-

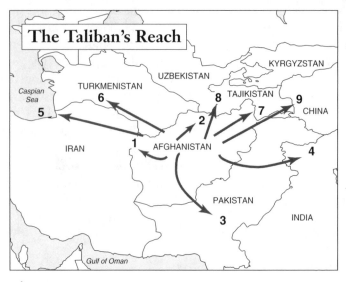

The Taliban's Reach

1 **Afghanistan-Iran border:** Troops deployed as tensions rise.
2 **Mazar-i-Sharif:** Thousands massacred as Taliban takes the city.
3 **Pakistan:** The Taliban's chief ally.
4 **Kashmir:** India fears Taliban will aid Muslims in fight for control.
5 **Caspian Sea:** Huge oil and gas deposits spur fight over pipeline routes.
6 **Turkmenistan:** Source of proposed pipeline across Afghanistan.
7 **Tajikistan:** Site of civil war between former Communists and Islamists.
8 **Uzbekistan and Tajikistan:** Key members of a group resisting radical Islam.
9 **Xinjiang-Uighur Autonomous Region:** Taliban successes spur on Muslim separatists.

ily planning is outlawed, women cannot be operated upon by a surgical team containing a male member), of the right to legal recourse (a woman's testimony is worth half a man's testimony; a woman cannot petition the court directly—this has to be done through a prescribed male member of her immediate family), of the right to recreation (all women's recreational and sporting facilities have been banned; women singers cannot sing lest their female voices "corrupt" males, etc.), and of the right to being human (they cannot show their faces in public to male strangers, they cannot wear bright coloured clothing, they cannot wear make-up, they can only appear outside their houses clad head to foot in shapeless bags called *burqas*, they cannot wear shoes with heels that click, lest the clicking sound of their feet corrupt males, they cannot travel in private vehicles with male passengers, they do not have the right to raise their voices when talking in public, they cannot laugh loud as it lures males into corruption, etc. etc.) . . .

Beating up of women for "disciplinary" reasons on the slightest pretext—wearing brightly-coloured shoes or thin stockings, having their bare ankles show when they walk, having their voices raised when they speak, having the sound of their laughter reach the ears of male strangers, having their heels click when walking, etc.—is a routine phenomenon in Afghanistan under the Taliban. Through such public beatings, which more often than not have resulted in death or disablement of the victim, the Taliban have cowed the civilian population into submission.

With the fundamentalists' war mentality, and fanned by ethnic hatred and religious bigotry, all areas that come under their control are regarded as occupied land and the inhabitants are treated accordingly. Sexual crimes against women, gang raping, lust murders, abductions of young females, [and] blackmail of families with eligible daughters were commonplace during the rule of the pre-Taliban fundamentalists. The Taliban initially made a show of piety and abhorring sexual crimes against women, but reports of their depravity are growing with each passing day. In this, like other atrocities, they have surpassed their fundamentalist brethren.

> "The Taliban's military prowess far exceeds
> their knowledge of Islam."

Fundamentalism in Afghanistan Is Not Islamic

Hassan Hathout

Hassan Hathout maintains in the following viewpoint that the Taliban, a so-called Islamic group that seized power of Afghanistan in 1996 and has since curtailed the rights of women, acts in complete opposition to the beliefs of Islam. Specifically, the Taliban's refusal to allow women an education defies the Qur'an's assertion that the pursuit of knowledge is obligatory for both genders. Hathout, a medical doctor, is the director of outreach at the Islamic Center of Southern California and the author of *Reading the Muslim Mind*.

As you read, consider the following questions:

1. What rights does Islam give women, according to the author?
2. What proof does Hathout offer that the Prophet Muhammad supported women's rights?

Reprinted, with permission, from Hassan Hathout, "Perspective on Women's Plight in Afghanistan" (1999), at the website of the Muslim Women's League, www.mwlusa.org.

Amerian Muslims were saddened and shocked by the news. This is one time we hoped it was just another example of the fabricated lies against Islam and Muslims. Reports sprinted through the air waves that upon the triumphant conquest of the capital of Afghanistan, Kabul, the Afghan Taliban ordered women out of school and out of their jobs and mandated men to grow a beard. More distressing was . . . that this was announced as a fulfillment of the teachings of Islam. Perhaps if the pretext was their own vision or the special brand of their culture, the concern would have fallen under the general umbrella of human rights, as indeed is the case. But when Islam is dragged into it, Muslims in particular should be specially involved.

In Defense of Islam

We feel it is our duty to defend the religion and defend its reputation, often tarnished by the Western media, but in this case, regrettably, by ill-advised Muslims. We go to great lengths educating people about what Islam really is; in this case, we have to educate all Muslims. And it is not, as you might think, that because we are American Muslims, our Islam must have been diluted and corrupted by the vagaries of Western life. Not at all. We are indeed Islam-abiding people, fairly conservative, and are blessed with Islamic scholarship that matches any elsewhere. And we enjoy a measure of freedom in living and expressing our religion that is not available in many so-called Muslim countries, even though we have our grievances and complaints.

The Taliban must know, as we do, that the Prophet [Muhammad] said, "The pursuit of knowledge is obligatory over every Muslim, male or female." Muslim women attained such scholarship that they became teachers to prominent men. Islam gave women the right to manage their wealth and generate income, and issued them the right of individual, independent ownership. The whole medical corps of the Prophet's army was an all-woman corps, and in some battles women took sword and shield and joined active combat, to be later praised by the Prophet. Women participated in public affairs, and it was the wisdom of Um-Salamah, the wife of the Prophet, that diffused the crisis amongst the

Muslims at the Hudaybiah treaty. Caliph Omar, the second successor to the Prophet as head of state, appointed a woman judge, Al-Shaffa, over commercial affairs. When Omar gave directives regarding the marriage dowry, it was a woman in the mosque who stood up to correct him by quoting the Quran, only for him to say, "The woman is right and I am wrong."

Islam Declared Gender Equality

To sweep away the pre-Islamic culture of ignorance that degraded the status of woman, Islam declared gender equality through the Prophet's words, "Women are the siblings of men." And when we come to the ultimate universal mission of the Muslim Umma (communities), i.e. enjoining good and forbidding evil, we find the Quran assigning it equally saying, "The believing men and women are the confidants to one another; they enjoin good and forbid evil."

It is a competitive world and fates of nations are being decided upon their acumen of knowledge and information. We cannot afford to continue to be parasites upon other nations, whether for the tank we drive or the loaf of bread we eat every day. In this respect we cannot just inactivate one half of our human resources. In some places in the Muslim world, women (and indeed men) are suppressed and denied their basic Islamic rights, but nothing to match the Taliban's recent decrees at the doorsteps of the 21st century.

Obviously, the Taliban's military prowess far exceeds their knowledge of Islam. When they fought the Russians, they captured our hearts and we invested so much hope in them. Our dreams were shattered as they emerged from their victory killing one another. Now the Taliban emerge victorious, but certainly Islam does not. Islam requires them to heal their enmities, build their country and clean it from hatred and prejudice, for this the razor that, as the Prophet said, does not shave hair, but shaves off religion.

Periodical Bibliography

The following articles have been selected to supplement the diverse views presented in this chapter. Addresses are provided for periodicals not indexed in the *Readers' Guide to Periodical Literature*, the *Alternative Press Index*, the *Social Sciences Index*, or the *Index to Legal Periodicals and Books*.

Valerie Ceccherini   "Rape and the Prophet," *Index on Censorship*, January/February 1999.

Jan Goodall   "Afghan Women Under the Taliban," *On the Issues*, Summer 1998.

Ellen Goodman   "Human Rights Violations Under the Taliban," *Liberal Opinion*, December 14, 1998. Available from PO Box 880, Vinton, IA 52349-0880.

Michael Griffin   "Hostages," *Index on Censorship*, March/April 1998.

Bob Herbert   "Fleeing the Taliban," *New York Times*, October 25, 1999.

Marvine Howe   "Turkey's Dilemma: What's on Women's Heads," *Ms.*, April/May 1999.

Douglas Jehl   "Arab Honor's Price: A Woman's Blood," *New York Times*, June 20, 1999.

Stephen Kinzer   "Musings on Freedom, by Wearer of Muslim Scarf," *New York Times*, May 12, 1999.

Judy Mabro   "Through a Veil Darkly," *Index on Censorship*, May/June 1998.

Shahrzad Mojab   "'Muslim' Women 'Western' Feminist: The Debate on Particulars and Universals," *Monthly Review*, December 1998.

Ahmar Mustikhan   "Women's Woes Under Islam," *World & I*, and Massoud Ansari   February 1998. Available from 3600 New York Ave. NE, Washington, DC 20002.

Seth Mydans   "Can She Run Indonesia? It's About Islam, or Is It?" *New York Times*, June 20, 1999.

Jane I. Smith   "Using Their Voice," *World & I*, September 1997.

Philip Taubman   "The Courageous Women of Iran," *New York Times*, December 26, 1997.

CHAPTER 3

Does Islam Promote Terrorism?

Chapter Preface

In a recent interview, *Time* magazine asked Osama bin Laden, leader of the fundamentalist group International Islamic Front for *Jihad*, whether he was responsible for the 1998 bombings of two U.S. embassies in Africa, which caused the deaths of over 200 people. Bin Laden responded by saying, "The International Islamic Front for *Jihad* against the U.S. and Israel has, by the grace of God, issued a crystal-clear *fatwa* [decree] calling on the Islamic nation to carry [out] *jihad* . . . If the instigation [of] *jihad* . . . is considered a crime, then let history be a witness that I am a criminal."

The term *jihad*, often translated as "holy war," is one of the most debated concepts of the Islamic faith. According to the Islamic holy book, the Qur'an, *jihad* is an obligation for all Muslims; the Qur'an's definition of *jihad*, however, is difficult to interpret. Based on bin Laden's use of the term, many Westerners contend that Islam is a power-seeking religion that requires its adherents to declare war on infidels.

Most Muslim-Americans, however, insist that fundamentalists such as bin Laden misrepresent the doctrine of *jihad*—which simply means "to strive for some objective." As one Muslim activist writes, "[*Jihad*] is a duty ['to enjoin good and forbid evil'] which is not exclusive to Muslims but applies to the human race. . . . *Jihad* is not a declaration of war against other religions—and certainly not against Christians and Jews. . . . Islam does not fight other religions."

The debate over the real meaning of *jihad* exacerbates the controversy over whether the Islam promotes terrorism, since commentators tend to adopt the definition that supports their views. The chapter that follows offers different perspectives on the definition of *jihad* and discusses whether the Islamic religion encourages its followers to engage in acts of violence and terrorism.

"*The primary terrorist threat to the United States comes from Islamic fundamentalists.*"

Islamic Terrorism Poses a Threat to the United States

Robert W. Tracinski

In the following viewpoint, Robert W. Tracinski argues that Islamic terrorism is a serious concern for the United States. In Tracinski's view, Islamic terrorism stems from a fundamental conflict between the values of Islam and those of Western civilization: Islamic fundamentalists use terrorism to express their hatred of America's secularism—the emphasis of worldly achievements over religion. Tracinski is the editor of the *Intellectual Activist* and a senior writer at the Ayn Rand Institute, a research group that works to uphold personal liberties and free market principles.

As you read, consider the following questions:
1. How does the author define the terms "secular" and "secularism"?
2. What examples does Tracinski provide of Islam's lapse into "primitive religious fanaticism"?
3. How does America stand as an affront to the outlook of Islamic fundamentalists, as explained by the author?

Reprinted, with permission, from Robert W. Tracinski, "Islam vs. the West," *The Intellectual Activist*, November 1998.

In response to the bombing of two US embassies by Islamic terrorists, our political and intellectual leaders have pursued an ideological campaign to exonerate the religion of Islam—the primary motivation of the terrorists—from any responsibility for terrorism. Just as the US policy in the realm of action has been one of conciliation toward our enemies (such as Iran), so the US policy in the realm of ideas has been to assert, in President Clinton's words, that there is no "inevitable clash between Western civilization and Western values and Islamic civilization and values."

The facts belie this view. The primary terrorist threat to the United States comes from Islamic fundamentalists—and the more fervent a country's or organization's Islamic beliefs, the more venomous are its denunciations of the West. This is not a coincidence. It stems directly from a fundamental ideological conflict between Islam and the West—an ideological conflict that can be seen, not only in the attacks by Islamic terrorists, but also in the near-civil-wars in countries like Turkey, Egypt, and Algeria between Islamic factions and their more-Westernized governments.

The Conflict Between Islam and the West

This central issue is the conflict between secularism and religious fundamentalism.

The *Webster's New World Dictionary* defines "secular" as: "of or relating to worldly things as distinguished from things relating to church and religion." "Secularism" is a cultural and intellectual doctrine, defined as "a worldly spirit, views, or the like; esp., a system of doctrines and practices that disregards or rejects any form of religious faith and worship," as well as a political doctrine: "the belief that religion and ecclesiastical affairs should not enter into the functions of the state." Defined in philosophic terms, secularism is the rejection of faith in favor of reason, the rejection of the supernatural in favor of pursuit of values in this world, and the rejection of theocracy in favor of separation of church and state.

This approach is embraced throughout the West and is even tolerated by the predominant Western religion, Christianity. Consider, for example, the recently published papal encyclical, *Fides et Ratio*, which appeals to the Thomist doctrine of a harmony between faith and reason. This view is an unstable compromise. Faith and reason are opposite methods—one consists of the rejection of evidence, while the other demands unwavering adherence to the evidence; ultimately, they cannot coexist in the same mind or in the same culture. But the papal encyclical is a timely reminder of the fundamental root of the West's secularism: Thomas Aquinas established the idea that reason is valid on its own terms, that it does not have to be subordinated to faith. His view laid the groundwork for the explosion of scientific and philosophic inquiry in the Renaissance and Enlightenment and made possible the increasing atrophy of religion in the West.

The Islamic World's Rejection of Reason

The Islamic world, by contrast, never had an Aquinas. Throughout the Middle Ages, the study of Greek and Roman science and philosophy had been more widespread in the Islamic world than in Europe. By the time of Aquinas, however, these philosophers were largely ignored and their works banned. While Europe experienced a Renaissance, the Islamic world rejected reason and science and lapsed back into primitive religious fanaticism. Hence, the present-day Islamic prohibitions on the education of women and on the free expression of ideas, as well as the strict Islamic code requiring women to keep their bodies covered (lest they should excite men's sexual desire), the prohibitions on alcohol, on music and art, and even (in some areas) on shaving or trimming one's beard—which is considered a worldly luxury. These religious prohibitions outlaw every manifestation of man's survival and happiness in this world.

America stands as a blatant affront to this fundamentalist outlook. Except for a few radical fundamentalists, Americans are secular; religion is not central to their lives. Predominantly, Americans embrace this-worldly values—wealth, physical beauty, sexual pleasure—and they base their intellectual and political institutions on rational debate and discussion. In the intellectual realm, even those who attack reason (such as [German philosopher Immanuel] Kant and his present-day followers in academia) usually do so, not by citing religious texts or the pronouncements of prophets, but

The Terrorist Threat from Islamic Leader Osama bin Laden

Osama bin Laden has declared war on the USA. Beginning in August 1996, and as recently as February 1999, he has issued *fatwas* (religious decrees) declaring *jihad* (holy war) against the USA. In both word and deed, he has made his hatred for the USA and the American people crystal clear. In numerous interviews he has said that he believes the USA is the enemy of Islam and has repeatedly stated that the USA must be evicted from Saudi Arabia and much of the Persian Gulf region. He is the prime suspect for the August 1998 US embassy bombings in East Africa and has threatened more terrorist attacks. Indeed, published reports suggest US intelligence agencies have disrupted at least seven planned bin Laden attacks between August 1998 and March 1999. Speaking of the August 1998 bombings of US embassies in Kenya and Tanzania, he told an interviewer: "Our job is to instigate [acts of terrorism] and by the grace of God, we did that, and certain people responded to this instigation."

Bin Laden has not only attacked US interests and threatened the USA and its citizens, he has raised the prospect of even more destructive future attacks with nuclear, chemical or biological weapons of mass destruction (WMD). Dale Watson, head of the FBI's foreign terrorism division, told an interviewer in late February that terrorists are actively pursuing WMD. Osama bin Laden certainly must have been one of the terrorists Watson had in mind. In fact, in a February 1999 interview, bin Laden said of his possible acquisition of WMD: "If I seek to acquire these weapons I am carrying out a duty." In February 1999, CIA director George Tenet told the Senate Armed Services Committee: "There is not the slightest doubt that Osama bin Laden, his worldwide allies and his sympathisers are planning further attacks against us." Tenet also expressed worry about "the serious prospect" that bin Laden could get access to chemical and biological weapons.

Stefan Leader, *Jane's Intelligence Review*, June 1, 1999.

by constructing pseudo-rational arguments for their positions. In the political realm, America has enshrined free speech as a centerpiece of its political system, allowing decisions to be determined, not by the decrees of religious leaders, but by the persuasion of voters and politicians through public debate.

"A Dangerous Example of Secular Values"

This is why America is the target of Islamic fundamentalists' venomous hatred. America represents a dangerous example of secular values—all the more dangerous because it is successful and powerful, and because it exerts that power over the Islamic world. America broadcasts television programs like "Baywatch" to the illegal satellite dishes of Iran; it harbors "blasphemous" writers like Salman Rushdie; and it uses its advanced technology to crush Iraqi soldiers in battle. Menachem Klein, an expert on Islam at Bar-Ilan University in Jerusalem, explains the conflict this way: "Islam puts God at its center. The Western world, on the other hand, is concerned with liberalism, freedom, and democracy. It's absolute heresy. And worst of all, from the Islamists' point of view, this culture is increasingly successful."

It is natural that the Islamic fundamentalists would choose terrorism as their means of striking back. Consistent with their rejection of reason and secular philosophy, they have no arguments to offer. They do not regard religious ideas as a matter for rational discussion, but as a matter of pure faith. Thus, they have no other alternative but to choose force and terror as a means to punish the "infidels"—literally, those "without faith."

There can be no compromise or friendly relations with those who hold this ideology in any form. But just as they refused to recognize the vicious nature of Communism and sought a policy of détente, so our leaders now refuse to recognize the vicious nature of Islam and its irreconcilable conflict with the West. To see what our leaders do not, Americans must reject both the "politically correct" dogma of "respecting all cultures" and the timid fear of offending anyone of any religion. Otherwise we will be doomed to continue our self-destructive policy of appeasement and conciliation toward those who wish to destroy us.

"*By now the media equate Islam with terror and fundamentalism, so that no matter where a bomb goes off in the world, the first suspects are always Muslims.*"

The Problem of Islamic Terrorism Is Overstated

Edward W. Said

Edward W. Said contends in the subsequent viewpoint that the threat of "Islamic terrorism" is little more than a smear campaign against the Islamic world—the new "official enemy" of the United States. As a result of the pernicious campaign waged by the U.S. and Israeli media, writes Said, Islam is unfairly associated with terrorism. Said, a professor at Columbia University, is the author of a number of books on Islam and the Middle East, including *Covering Islam: How the Media and Experts Determine How We See the Rest of the World, After the Last Sky: Palestinian Lives,* and *Out of Place: A Memoir.*

As you read, consider the following questions:

1. What is the background of the U.S. campaign against Islam, in Said's view?
2. What is the basic underlying premise of the policies of the U.S. and Israel toward Islam, as stated by the author?
3. According to Said, what status has the word "Islamic" acquired in the media?

Excerpted from Edward W. Said, "Declaring War on Islam," *The Progressive*, May 1996. Reprinted by permission of the author.

I srael and the United States, deliberately using the weapons of mass media, psychological warfare, and political pressure, have . . . been leading a campaign against Islam (with Iran as its main agent) as the origin of terror and "fundamentalism."

Consider the background. Ever since the collapse of the Soviet Union there has been an active, explicit search in the United States for new official enemies, a search that has now come to settle on "Islam" as a manufactured opponent. In 1991 the *Washington Post* leaked news of a continuing study in the U.S. defense and intelligence establishment of the need to find such an enemy: Even then, Islam was the candidate.

True, there are ancient rivalries between the West and Islam, and there has been a massive amount of rhetoric in the Islamic, especially Arab, world against the West, plus a whole array of parties, leaders, and ideological trends for whom the Great Satan is the United States as the West's repulsive embodiment. In addition, recent bloodshed in Algeria, Sudan, Egypt, Syria, and Iraq—where one source of conflict is a brutalizing manipulation of religion—has totally corrupted the Arab world's civil life.

The Western Assault on the Islamic World

But this has to be seen along with the long history of imperial Western intervention in the Islamic world, the continued assault upon its culture and traditions as a standard feature of academic and popular discourse, and (perhaps most important) the frank disdain with which the wishes and aspirations of Muslims, but particularly Arabs, are treated.

There are now American and Israeli armies settled on Arab soil, but no Arab or Muslim armies in the West; few Arabs or Muslims in the West feel like anything except hated terrorists. Official Israeli discourse has taken advantage of all this. During the 1970s it was a staple of Israeli foreign-affairs jargon that Palestinians were always to be identified with terrorism. Now, in the same cynical and calculated manner, both Israel and the United States identify fundamentalist Islam—a label that is often compressed into the one word "Islam"—with opposition to the peace process, to Western interests, to democracy, and to Western civilization.

I do not want to be understood as saying that all this

111

amounts to a conspiracy, although I do think that there is active collusion between Israel and the United States in terms of planning, conceptualization, and now, since Sharm al Sheikh [Middle East Peace Summit, held in Sharm-al-Sheikh, Egypt, on March 13, 1996], grand strategy. What they both want is compliance: in effect, an Islamic and Arab world that has simply resigned itself (as many of its leaders already have) to the dictates of the Pax Americana-Israelica.

In my opinion, one can only obey such dictates as these; one cannot have a dialogue with them, since according to their most basic underlying premise, the grand strategy regards Muslims and Arabs as fundamentally delinquent. Only when Muslims totally fall into line, speak the same language, take the same measures as Israel and the United States do, can they be expected to be "normal," at which point of course they are no longer really Arab and Muslim. They have simply become "peace-makers." What a pity that so noble an idea as "peace" has become a corrupted embellishment of power masquerading as reconciliation.

The "Islamic Threat"

U.S. cultural institutions are trumpeting the "Islamic threat." Many of the authoritative foreign-policy institutions, journals, and newspapers of record have held symposia, published articles, and released studies proclaiming it. In addition, feature films as well as television documentaries have hyped the threat.

Judith Miller, among several others, is one of the leaders of the journalistic effort; Bernard Lewis and his students lead the so-called scholarly effort. Samuel Huntington's famous article on the clash of civilizations put forward the much-debated thesis that certain civilizations are incompatible with the West, Islamic civilization being the central instance. Finally, the Fundamentalism Project of the American Academy of Arts and Sciences has made Islam the preferred candidate for demon status in its study; both Jewish and Christian, to say nothing of Slavic or Hindu, fundamentalism get very little comparative attention.

By now the media equate Islam with terror and fundamentalism, so that no matter where a bomb goes off in the world, the first suspects are always Muslims and/or Arabs.

The word "Islamic" itself has acquired the bristling status of a frightening, irrational monster. Every article published about Hamas or Islamic fundamentalism or Iran—about which it is now impossible to speak rationally—describes an ahistorical world of pure despotism, pure rage, pure violence, all of it in some way targeting "us," a group of innocent victims who happen to ride buses or go about some harmless daily business, unconnected with the decades of suffering imposed on an entire people.

Chris Britt. Reprinted by permission of Copley News Service.

There is never an indication at all that for centuries there has been one form or another of Western infringement directed against the land and peoples of Islam. Long articles by instant experts create the impression that Hamas flourishes gratuitously, or because of Iran, for no other ascertainable reason at all, except to attack Jews and the West. Few of those who fulminate against terrorism mention the occupation, or the constant attacks on Arabs and Muslims.

In 1996, the veteran French journalist Eric Rouleau appeared on a national TV program with the former head of the CIA, James Woolsey, and Geoffrey Kemp, a so-called terrorism expert. Kemp and Woolsey were asked by the moderator about the Sharm al-Sheikh summit and both spoke with great effusiveness about its value. Rouleau tried three times to explain the "context" that produced Hamas, but the moderator never gave him a chance to say a word. All anyone wanted was proof that "we" were opposing Islamic terrorism and feeling good about it. Moreover, no one bothered to point out that Hamas's quarrel with the "peace process" has from the beginning been advanced on nationalist, not Islamic, principles.

A Declaration of War Against Non-Western Civilizations

Thus Huntington's thesis—which in my opinion amounts to a blanket declaration of war against all civilizations that do not conform to Western values—is now being put into effect.

The worst aspect of all this is that the U.S.-Israeli strategy is turning Arab governments into collaborators in the effort against an ever-increasing number of their own people. I am not sure how many are conscious of this process, but I am certain it is happening.

On a popular level, the policy threatens to rob us of our memory and of our past, so that we will be faced with the choice of coming into the American fold, which humanly offers very little (the terribly compromised peace process is one reward), or of remaining outside, stripped of everything except the terrorist-fundamentalist identity and therefore subject to intimidation, boycott, and perhaps even extermination.

"Jihad has principally one meaning: a military action designed to expand the outer borders of the realm of Islam."

The Islamic Doctrine of *Jihad* Advocates Violence

Raphael Israeli

In the subsequent viewpoint, Raphael Israeli argues that the doctrine of *jihad*—the Islamic belief that Muslims should use force to expand and defend their religion—inspires the terrorist acts of radical Islamic groups. According to Israeli, the philosophy of *jihad* encourages Muslims to view non-Muslims as enemies who need to be conquered and motivates terrorist fanatics to sacrifice their lives for the cause of Islam. Israeli is a professor of Islamic and Chinese Studies at the Hebrew University of Jerusalem. He is the author of several books about Middle Eastern affairs, including *Muslim Fundamentalism in Israel* and *Fundamentalist Islam and Israel.*

As you read, consider the following questions:
1. As stated by Israeli, what accusations does Islamic leader Sayyid Qutb make against the Jews and how are those accusations echoed by the Islamic group Hamas?
2. According to Israeli, what is the duty of all Muslims under the doctrine of *jihad*?
3. Why has *jihad* become the rallying slogan of radical Islamic groups, in the author's opinion?

Excerpted from Raphael Israeli, "Islamikaze and Their Significance," *Terrorism and Political Violence*, vol. 9, no. 3 (Autumn 1997), published by Frank Cass & Company, 900 Eastern Ave., Ilford, Essex, England. Copyright Frank Cass & Co., Ltd. Reprinted by permission of the publisher.

Radical Islamic movements in general have clearly identified their enemy: the regimes in the Islamic world which practice non-Islamic law; the West which has been undermining Islam from within and corrupting it with its norms of permissiveness in order to totter it and replace it; and Israel-Zionism—the Jews, who are intrinsically the enemies of Allah and humanity, in addition to their being an arm of the West in the heart of the Islamic world. The enemy must be depicted in evil terms so as to make it a free prey for Muslims to attack and destroy. Rhetorical delegitimation of their enemy is an essential step towards making the use of violence permissible, even desirable, against him. Hence the systematic and virulent onslaughts of those movements against what they perceive as their enemies, domestic and external.

In the early 1950s, Sayyid Qutb, one of the great masters of radical Islam, published his book *Our Campaign Against the Jews* where he warned of their evil subversion of Islam, and urged Muslims to go back to the Qur'an lest Islam might be destroyed. Qutb described at length the Jewish propensity for plotting, for turning their backs on their own leaders, for hostility towards their prophets, for rebelling against Divine Will, for concocting revolutions and trouble everywhere, for instigating war and destruction, etc. He accused them of being egotistic and ungrateful, of having forged their holy scriptures, and claimed that their innate hatred towards Islam stemmed from their hostility to the angel Gabriel who transmitted the Holy Revelation of the Qur'an to the Prophet of Islam.

Those very attacks against the Jews are echoed, almost *verbatim*, by the Charter of the Hamas published in 1988:

The Nazism of the Jews does not skip women and children. . . .They make war against people's livelihood, plunder their money and threaten their honour. In their horrible actions they mistreat people like the most horrendous war criminals. . . .

The enemies have been scheming for a long time. . . .They accumulated a huge and influential material wealth which they put to the service of implementing their dream: to take control of the world media and news agencies, the press, publishing houses, broadcasting and the like . . . they stood behind the French and Communist Revolutions and most of the revolutions we hear about. They used their money to establish clandestine organisations which are spreading around the world in order to destroy societies and carry out Zionist interests. Such organisations are: the Free Masons, Rotary Clubs, Lions Clubs, B'nai Brith and the like. All of them are subversive spying organisations. They also influenced imperialistic states and made them colonise many countries in order to exploit the wealth of those countries and spread their corruption therein. . . .

The Muslim radical bent on violence finds the recipe for how to act against this abominable enemy in the form of a Hadith [traditions or sayings attributed to the prophet Muhammad] related to the Prophet:

> The Time [of Resurrection] will not come until Muslims will fight against the Jews [and kill them], until the Jews hide behind rocks and trees which will cry: O Muslim! There is a Jew hiding behind me, come on and kill him. . . .

Similarly, regimes in the Islamic world which are termed 'heretic' by the fundamentalists can become the target of the same kind of hatred and violence.

The Doctrine of *Jihad*

The underlying justification to launch war against such evil enemies, domestic and external, is distilled in the quintessential notion of *jihad*. Etymologically, this word was meant to designate an intellectual 'striving', and by extension also a physical striving, for a cause. In Islamic *shari'a* [law], however, *jihad* has principally one meaning: a military action designed to expand the outer borders of the realm of Islam or to protect the borders of *dar al-Islam* (Pax Islamica) from encroaching Unbelievers. This idea is founded on the notion that Islam is not simply one of the revealed religions, but the prevailing faith which has come to replace the other monotheistic religions, it being the latest divine revelation, and therefore the most updated (as it were).

It is then incumbent upon Islam to extend its rule all over the world by peaceful means if possible, by war if necessary. *Jihad* is usually viewed as a collective duty (*Fard kifaya*) binding the Muslim community, the *umma*, as a whole. Namely, when the Muslim authorities-that-be pursue *jihad*, every Muslim individual is thereby viewed as having discharged his duty. The duty to fight *jihad* is universal and perpetual until the entire world comes under Muslim dominion. However, because Muslim countries have desisted in practice, under various theological and pragmatic considerations, from this idea, which otherwise would have permanently pitted them against the rest of the world, Muslim fundamentalists, the Islamikaze [Islamic suicide-bombers] included, have come to take this duty as a personal one *(Fard 'ayn)*, and so have consecrated any struggle of theirs against non-believers as a pursuit of that holy duty. Let us listen to what the Hamas group has to say in this regard:

> When our enemies usurp our Islamic lands, *Jihad* becomes a duty binding on all Muslims. In order to face the usurpation of Palestine by the Jews, we have no escape from raising the

---

One *Jihad* Warrior in Afghanistan

Abdul Qudoos . . . was unlike the stereotype of a hardened Afghan warrior. No blood in the eyes, no wavy beard—only a stiff mustache.

He was nine years old when his family fled to Pakistan after the Soviet invasion of Afghanistan in 1979. Like most Afghan refugee boys, Abdul Qudoos was educated and trained in guerrilla warfare at a religious seminary, or madrisa. Four years later, he was back in his native country, fighting the communists.

"For five years I was part of the *jihad*. And when it was over and the civil war started, my father advised me not to use my arms against my erstwhile brothers-in-arms. So I returned to Pakistan," he said, as he puffed on his cigarette.

"But I don't know any other way of life. Martyrdom is the goal of my life. You die, anyway. It's better to be killed fighting in the way of Allah than to shrink yourself to death in bed," he said, explaining his decision to go to Kashmir and become a "freedom fighter" against Indian troops.

Abdul Qudoos belonged to one of the many *jihadi* networks that evolved during the Afghan war, fighting with the political, financial, and military support of the United States, whose objective of bringing down the "Evil Empire" was duly achieved. But the struggle left behind an entire generation of men whose sole aim in life is to fight until "the final victory of Islam"—Islam as they understand it—is achieved.

Najum Mushtaq, *Bulletin of the Atomic Scientists*, July/August 1999.

---

banner of *Jihad*. This would require the propagation of Islamic consciousness among the masses on all local, Arab and Islamic levels. We must spread the spirit of *Jihad* among the Islamic *umma*, clash with the enemies and join the ranks of *Jihad* fighters.

According to this view, and along the lines charted by Sayyid Qutb and others before him, the Hamas view the war against Israel and the Jews as a religious war, therefore Muslims ought to mobilise and swell their ranks and fight it to the finish, whatever the price. For, as one of their leaflets put it, 'Our struggle with the Jews is a struggle between Truth and emptiness, between Islam and Judaism'. Sheikh Tamimi, one of the leading founders of the Islamic Jihad group, published a booklet entitled *The Obliteration of Israel: a Qur'anic Imperative*. Moved by the sheikh's vow that 'we shall not accede to a Jewish state on our land, even if it is only one village', young Palestinians joined his organisation and were prepared to put their lives on the line for what they saw as a divine command. Thus, the Jihad group recruited resolute Islamikaze who embarked on operations designed to inflict on the enemy as many casualties as possible, often without planning their own escape. For example, during the Gulf War, one Jihad recruit, instructed to set up and detonate a car-bomb on a busy street in one of the countries fighting against Iraq, told a *Times* correspondent that the fate he awaited in the afterworld was far superior to the 'rotten life he had at present'. But he added that his life was not all that miserable, for he was readying himself to die for his cause. He said that all lives were moving towards Heaven or Hell, and he chose Heaven.

Jihad Is Violent

In spite of the wide variety of interpretations given to *jihad* in modern times, some of which are soft and subtle, it is evident that the Muslim radicals, including Islamic Jihad, the Hamas, the Hizballah, and certainly the Islamikaze among them, are uncompromisingly dedicated to the violent brand thereof. They refer to many Qur'anic passages which assure the martyr (that is, the dead in the course of *jihad*), all manner of rewards in the next world.

This is the reason why *jihad* has become the rallying slogan of many of those radical movements, as in 'Allah is the goal, the Prophet the model, the Qur'an the Constitution, Jihad the path, and death for the cause of Allah the most sublime creed' [a slogan of Hamas]. Death in the course of *jihad* becomes, then, an expected and even desirable outcome, especially when *jihad* is taken as the explanatory motive of history. Indeed, radical Islamic movements regard the present generation's struggle in the path of Allah as only one link in the chain of continuous *jihad*, inasmuch as precedent fighters/martyrs had opened the path and the living in each generation must follow in their footsteps, 'whatever time it might take'. In fact, the Muslim Brothers' symbol is constituted by a Qur'an Book surrounded by two swords, their explication being that force (*jihad* by the sword) defends justice as encapsulated in the Qur'an.

Hence the powerful appeal for *jihad*, and for death in *jihad* if necessary, is reinforced by the Islamic legal prescription that all are liable to *jihad* except for the blind, the handicapped and the old, who cannot expend the requisite effort in the battlefield. In the macho-prone youth of the Islamic world, going to *jihad* is proof that one is not afflicted by those inabilities, Allah Forbid! One of the heads of the Muslim Brothers in Egypt called upon the *jihad* fighters to brandish the banner of the Holy War until all Islamic lands are liberated and the Islamic state is reinstituted. Similarly, Hamas leaders have repeatedly emphasised the importance of *jihad* by according to it the validity of a sixth Pillar. [There are five pillars, or tenets, of Islam.] In a *fatwa* [religious decree] circulated in the territories under Israeli rule, spiritual leaders of the Palestinians have indeed determined that *jihad* is a personal duty binding on each and every individual 'until the usurper has been removed from the land by force of the sword'. They rejected peace with Israel, if only because that would amount to cessation of the *jihad* and the obstruction of the road of *jihad* before the coming generations.

"Jihad *is a duty of Muslims to commit themselves to a struggle on all fronts—moral, spiritual and political—to create a just and decent society.*"

The Islamic Doctrine of *Jihad* Does Not Advocate Violence

Mohammed Abdul Malek

Mohammed Abdul Malek, author of *A Study of the Qur'an: The Universal Guidance for Mankind*, a book explaining the beliefs of Islam, contends in the following viewpoint that *jihad* is a misunderstood concept in Islam. Contrary to the commonly held belief that *jihad* exhorts Muslims to expand Islam by violent means, Malek claims that *jihad* simply refers to a spiritual striving to attain nearness to Allah. The doctrine of *jihad* never encourages war or violence, he maintains.

As you read, consider the following questions:

1. What evidence does Malek provide that *jihad* does not mean "war"?
2. As cited by the author, what is the definition of *jihad* provided by Ibrahim Golightly?
3. What evidence does Malek provide that what the *jihad* carried out against unbelievers and hypocrites was not a war?

Excerpted from Mohammed Abdul Malek, *A Study of the Qur'an: The Universal Guidance for Mankind*, at http://members.aol.com/Mamalek1/ch8s8.htm. Reprinted by permission of the author.

A great deal of misconception exists, particularly in the West, with regard to the meaning of the word *Jihad* in Islam. In reality *jihad* is a duty of Muslims to commit themselves to a struggle on all fronts—moral, spiritual and political—to create a just and decent society. It is not a 'holy war' against the non-believers as is commonly understood. The phrase 'holy war' was coined by the West in its struggle against the Muslims during the time of the Crusades (a war instigated by the Church for religious gain). There are other words in Arabic which are more appropriate to use in a war situation, if war was the principal purpose of *Jihad*. Examples of such words are *harb* (war) and *ma'araka* (battle). The Qur'an could have used these instead of *Jihad*, if the intention was the declaration of war. Here I find it very useful to quote from *Haji* Ibrahim Golightly as he was answering a question on *Jihad*. I quote the section where he was clarifying the meaning of *Jihad*:

> *Jihad* means to strive or make an effort, usually in an Islamic context, so that anything which requires an effort to be made is *Jihad* and the person doing it is a *mujahid*. The media would have us believe that it is fighting and killing in the name of Allah. It is certainly in the name of Allah, but, as usual, the media have corrupted the meaning so that they can apply its new meaning to 'fundamentalist Muslims', basically any Muslim who does not subscribe totally to the Western way of life. Making time in a busy schedule to study the Qur'an; going to a *halal* butcher rather than the closest or most convenient one; discussing Islam with both Muslims and non-Muslims and helping them to understand it better; studying ayat (signs), both of Qur'an and in nature and science, in order to increase *ilm*, or knowledge; setting other Muslims a good example and showing non-Muslims the true way of Muslims; are all examples of *Jihad* in daily life. *Jihad* is the effort made, not just against internal and external evils, but also to live at peace with oneself and one's community (Muslim and non-Muslim).

Finally he concluded his answer by saying: "simply explaining the true meaning of *Jihad* to those who do not know, is *Jihad* in itself".

Jihad Must Be Judged in Context

In fact, the implication of the word *Jihad*, like all other words, can only be judged in the context of the Qur'anic verses in

The Real Meaning of *Jihad*

Jihad basically means striving and refers to the unceasing effort an individual must make towards self-improvement and self-purification. It also refers to the duty of Muslims, at both the individual and collective level, to struggle against all forms of evil, corruption, injustice, tyranny and oppression—whether this injustice is committed against Muslims or non-Muslims.

Muslimsonline.com, "Jihad—In the Quran and Sunnah."

---

which it is used. The following are some typical verses, with appropriate comments, to indicate what the Qur'an implies by *Jihad*. The material below, including most of the translations, are based on Maulana Muhammad Ali's book *The Religion of Islam*.

(22:78) And strive hard (*jahidu*) for Allah with the endeavour which is right.

The *jihad* implies that one should exert one's self to the utmost ability, i.e moral, spiritual or political, for the cause of Allah; to establish Allah's *Deen*, without resorting to war.

(29:6) And whoever strives hard (*jahada*), he strives (*yujahidu*) only for his own soul, that is for his own benefit, for Allah is altogether Independent of (His) creatures.

(29:69) And those who strive hard (*jahadu*) for Us, We will certainly guide them in Our ways, and Allah is surely with the doers of good.

A Spiritual Striving

The Arabic word *jahadu* is derived from *jihad*, and the addition of *fi-na* (for Us) shows, that *jihad*, in this case, is the spiritual striving to attain nearness to Allah, and the result of this *jihad* is stated to be Allah's guidance for those striving in His ways.

(25:52) So do not follow the unbelievers and strive hard (*jahid*) against them a mighty striving (*jihad-un*) with it.

The personal pronoun 'it' refers clearly to the Qur'an, as the context shows. It is a struggle (*jihad*) to win over the unbelievers, not of the sword but of the Qur'an.

(66:9) O Prophet! Strive (*jahade*) against the disbelievers and the hypocrites, and be stern with them. . . .

Jihad Does Not Imply War

Here the Prophet is asked to carry on a *jihad* against both unbelievers and hypocrites. The hypocrites were those who were outwardly Muslims and lived among Muslims, and were treated like Muslims in all respects. They came to the mosque and prayed with the Muslims. A war against them was unthinkable and none was ever undertaken. They sometimes fought along with the Muslims against the unbelievers. Therefore the injunction to carry on a *jihad* against both the unbelievers and hypocrites could not mean the waging of war against them. It was a *jihad* in the same sense in which the word is used in the above verses, a *jihad* carried on by means of the Holy Qur'an as expressly stated in 25:52, a striving hard to win them over to Islam. Therefore *jihad* in both 25:52 and 66:9 is used in the moral and political sense. Again, *it does not imply war.*

(2:218) Lo! Those who believe, and those who emigrate (to escape the persecution) and strive hard (*jahadu*) in the way of Allah, these have hope of Allah's mercy. Allah is Forgiving and Merciful.

(8:74) Those who believed and left their homes and strove hard (*jahadu*) for the cause of Allah, and those who took them in and helped them—these are the believers in truth. For them is pardon, and a bountiful provision.

(3:142) Or deemed ye that ye would enter Paradise while yet Allah knoweth not those of you who strive hard (*jahadu*), nor knoweth those (of you) who are steadfast?

In all these verses *jihad* is used in the general sense of striving hard, morally, spiritually, and in our day to day life. In all cases *jihad* implies a struggle in Allah's ways to achieve an objective, without resorting to war.

> *"The portrayal of Arab Muslims over the past 30 years—in our cartoons and films as well as words—has reached Nazi-like proportions."*

The Media Stereotype Muslims as Terrorists

Robert Fisk

Robert Fisk, a journalist who writes for the British *Independent*, maintains in the following viewpoint that Western media promulgate demeaning stereotypes about Muslims. Fisk argues that Muslims, especially Arab Muslims, are consistently stereotyped in films, television programs, cartoons—and even the news—as "terrorist animals" who have no regard for human life. Although Islamic groups are not without their faults, he writes, Muslims certainly do not deserve to be the targets of racist propaganda.

As you read, consider the following questions:
1. What evidence does Fisk provide that the media's portrayal of Arab-Americans "has reached Nazi-like proportions"?
2. What are the expressions commonly used about Arabs in Hollywood movies, according to the investigation conducted by Professor Jack Shaheen?
3. How does the media stereotype Muslims as terrorists, according to the author?

Reprinted from Robert Fisk, "The West's Fear of Islam Is No Excuse for Racism," *The Independent*, November 3, 1999, p. 5, with permission. Copyright Newspaper Publishing PLC.

On a rainy summer afternoon in 1992, a certain Colonel Popovic welcomed me to the notorious concentration camp at Manjaca [where Bosnian Muslims were held by Serbs in the former Yugoslavia] with a question. "Do you know what jihad is?" he roared. My heart sank. He could have stepped out of any Hollywood movie or Western newspaper report, let alone from the heart of Serbian nationalism. Inside Manjaca were the "ethnically cleansed" Muslim survivors of north-western Bosnia. But listening to Colonel Popovic, I reflected I had heard the same pernicious, insidious words used about Arab Muslims in the Middle East.

A reporter is uniquely positioned to observe the cancer of racism. Just a year later, I was in southern Lebanon, interviewing hundreds of Palestinian Hamas members who had been illegally deported from Israel and the occupied territories and marooned on a mountainside inside Lebanon. Most of them were intelligent men, some with university degrees, several educated in Britain. They were against the "peace process", but only a few of them believed violence could achieve their ends. A week later, I was back in Bosnia where, on CNN, I heard them described as "extremists". A further three weeks later in the California resort of Pismo Beach, I was watching the American CBS television channel and there were the same Palestinians on their cold mountainside, this time described as "suspected terrorists".

Pismo Beach was an ironic place to witness this transformation of humans into potential beasts. For it was on the sands here that Hollywood first immortalised the Arab as a heroic son of the desert. This was where Rudolph Valentino made *The Sheikh*, where the Arab was defined as a romantic, courageous figure in the third decade of the century. Unfortunately, you only have to watch the scratched old movie to realise that Sheikh Ahmed is not an Arab. "His father was an Englishman," says the script. "His mother a Spaniard." So that's all right then.

How the West Demeans and Stereotypes Muslims

In the sublimely neutral countryside of Ditchley Park [in Oxfordshire, England], some of the great and the good will be gathering to debate how we in the West have demeaned, stereotyped and racially abused Muslims in our press, television and cinema. Prince Abdullah of Saudi Arabia, former US ambassador Edward Djerejian, Arab editor Khaled al-Maeena, Rabbi Neuberger and sundry diplomats and journalists will spend three days discussing the ever-more dangerous "Islamo-phobia" that is currently infecting our reporting and vision of the Muslim world—and especially of the Middle East.

They will have a lot to talk about. For the portrayal of Arab Muslims over the past 30 years—in our cartoons and films as well as words—has reached Nazi-like proportions. Greedy, hook-nosed, vicious, violent, rapacious, turbaned or "kaffiyehed" Iranians and Arabs have replaced the cartoon Jews of *Volkischer Beobachter* [a Nazi newspaper that published anti-Semitic propaganda] or *Der Ewige Jude* ["The Eternal Jew," a hate-propaganda film created by the Nazis]. I had just arrived in the Middle East more than 20 years ago when I first saw, on television, the movie *Ashanti*. It starred Omar Sharif and Roger Moore and portrayed Arabs as slave traders, murderers, child-molesters and sadists. The film was, said the credits, partly made on location in Israel.

I was stunned. No wonder so many reports spoke of Arabs as "terrorists". No wonder so many editorials referred to "terrorist animals". And the more films I watched, the more cartoons I saw, the more editorials I read, the more our fear of the despicable, fearful, alien Muslim seemed to be spreading. If the Nazis could portray the Jews as sub-humans who threatened Western "civilisation" and "culture" so could we portray Muslims as sinister, evil, over-breeding and worthy of destruction.

How come, I asked myself, that a Palestinian who murdered innocent Israelis was in our reports a "terrorist"—which he surely was—while an Israeli who murdered 29 innocent Palestinians in a Hebron mosque was merely an "extremist", a "zealot" or (my favourite) "a member of the Jewish underground"? How come a Hizbullah guerrilla fighting Israeli occupation forces in Lebanon was an "Islamic fundamentalist" while Croatian or Serb killers in Bosnia were not "Christian fundamentalists"? Even our most right-wing newspapers refer to "IRA terrorists" rather than "Catholic terrorists". How come an Arab who threatens America (Ossama bin Laden) is a "super-terrorist", but an Israeli who murders his own prime minister is just a "fanatic"?

Hollywood's Portrayal of Muslims

Who laid these ground rules, these vicious double standards? You only have to go to Hollywood to understand part of the answer. *Navy SEALS*, *True Lies*, *Broadcast News*, *Delta Force*, even *The American President*—remember the Arab "terrorist" attack on US forces in Israel which leads "our" president to launch an assault on Libya?—are only a few of the dozens of movies to portray Arab Muslims or Iranians as a hateful, cruel people.

An investigation by Professor Jack Shaheen of Southern Illinois University provides a list of expressions used about Arabs in Hollywood movies (most of which have been widely shown in Britain), including "scumbag", "son-of-a-bitch", "a fly in a piece of shit", "animals", "bastards", "sucking pigs", "stateless savages", "desert skunks" and, of course, "terrorists". Cartoons and American papers routinely show Arabs as virtual animals.

In 1996, the *Miami Herald* pictured a bearded ape creature with "Islam" on his turban, saying "We bomb innocent women and children to smithereens". Two days after the bombing of the World Trade Centre—a wicked act that was indeed carried out by Muslims—the *New York Post* carried a cartoon of the Statue of Liberty with this distorted version of its poem: "Give us your tired, your poor, your huddled masses, your terrorists, your murderers, your slime, your evil cowards, your religious fanatics . . ."

Blaming Muslim "Terrorists"

Needless to say, when Americans bombed the Oklahoma government building, Muslim "terrorists" were the first to be blamed. "In the name of Islam", one of Rupert Murdoch's US papers headlined over a picture of a dead child. Even in Britain, we did the same. Bernard Levin wrote that: "As for Oklahoma, it will be called Khartoum on the Mississippi, and woe betide anyone who calls it anything else." Once the culprits turned out to be Americans, the word "terrorism" faded from the headlines. They were "fanatics". A similar transformation occurred when the "terrorist" bombing of a TWA flight turned out to be a disaster probably caused by a technical fault.

Turbaned mullahs became stock figures in British cartoons from the Seventies—especially in *Punch*. By 1992, the *Times* could show a Muslim wiping his bloodied sabre on a union flag while an innocent woman lay dead behind him. The Rushdie affair [the publication of Salman Rushdie's novel, *The Satanic Verses*, which criticized Islam, led to Islamic calls for his execution] brought forth a contagion of such images while journalists and political leaders warned us of the dangers of a coming war with Islam. "Muslim fundamentalism" announced NATO secretary general Willy Claes in 1995, "is at least as dangerous as communism once was. . . . It represents terrorism, religious fanaticism."

The Effect of Negative Media Stereotypes on Muslims

Negative imagery of Muslims and Islam has a very real effect on the daily lives of Muslims who choose to call North America their home. It ranges from annoying jokes, to discrimination in employment and education, to the more serious incidents of hate crimes. Consider how [in 1995], North America's 6 million Muslims, including their 350,000 coreligionists in Canada, were immediately assumed guilty in the Oklahoma City bombing by the media. The Washington-based Council on American-Islamic Relations (CAIR) issued a report recently, called *A Rush to Judgment*, detailing more than 200 incidents of anti-Muslim threats, harassment, stereotyping, property damage and physical assaults resulting from unfounded links between Muslims and the April 19, 1995, terrorist attack on the federal building in Oklahoma City. We were vilified publicly, harassed, beaten and our houses of worship vandalized. In Oklahoma City, a Muslim woman suffered a miscarriage during her eighth month of pregnancy when hate-mongers attacked her home in the wake of the tragic bombing.

Sheema Khan, *The Gazette*, April 24, 1996.

Yes, I know the Arabs can be their own worst enemies. They have produced some truly grotesque dictators and their violent groups have committed some evil deeds in the name of Islam. It didn't need 23 years in the Arab world to make me rage about those puritanical, infantile clerics—Christian as well as Muslim or Jew—who refuse to see that the world is a complex society worthy of compassion as well as dogma. And in the Cairo press, Jews are often pictured in top hats with money bags—the classic Nazi image—although it was a Jewish-American friend who lamented to me the other day about the number of anti-Arab cartoons and films produced by Jewish Americans.

So the Ditchley conference will have plenty to discuss. It should not forget the flaws of Muslim societies or the cruelty of Arab regimes. Guests should remember how seriously—and rightly so—we regard any racial or anti-Semitic slur against Jews. But I wonder if they should not also ask themselves whether it is time to show the same sensitivity, the same concern and—given the fact that Arabs are also a Semitic people—the same hatred of racism when Muslims of the Middle East are portrayed in the same manner that Hitler used for the doomed Jews of Europe.

> "*Films . . . are not the arbiters of the image of Muslims in America. How Muslims respond to their stereotypes is what defines their image.*"

Media Stereotypes Do Not Define the Image of Muslims

Kazim Saeed

Responding to arguments that the media unfairly portrays Muslims as terrorists, Kazim Saeed contends in the following viewpoint that media stereotypes do not define the image of Muslims; in fact, he proposes, the reactions of Muslims to media stereotypes say more about Muslims than the stereotypes themselves. Instead of complaining about media caricatures, Saeed writes, Muslims should focus their attention on veritable issues of concern, such as U.S. foreign policy toward Muslim countries. At the time this viewpoint was written, Saeed was a graduate student at Princeton University's Woodrow Wilson School of Public and International Affairs.

As you read, consider the following questions:
1. On what basis does Saeed assert that the stereotype of Muslims as terrorists "is not a concoction"?
2. What should be the critical political objective of American Muslims, according to Saeed?
3. How does "whining" alter the stereotype of Muslims, in the author's view?

Reprinted, with permission, from Kazim Saeed, "Muslims Should Take Control of Their Own Image and Stereotypes," *Earth Times*, Arts and Cultures section, November 24, 1998.

Muslim terrorism against the United States seems to have succeeded in terrorizing American Muslims more than anyone else. *The Siege*, a Hollywood thriller about Muslim terrorism in New York, brought Muslim groups out for another public cry against the stereotyping of Muslims. By manifesting this response in protests, on editorial pages, and at public debates, American Muslims are harming their image rather than improving it.

Edward Zwick, director of *The Siege*, says the film dispels stereotypes about Muslims. The Council on American-Islamic Relations says the film reinforces the stereotypes and increases the probability of random violence against Muslims. Invariably, films like *The Siege* are not the arbiters of the image of Muslims in America. How Muslims respond to their stereotypes is what defines their image. American Muslims continue to miss this point as they carve out their place in the American polity.

Examining Stereotypes About Muslims

Unfair or not, the stereotype is not a concoction. Exactly a year before the release of *The Siege*, Yousef Ramzi and Aimal Kansi were convicted by US courts for acts of terrorism. Ramzi admitted to his lead role in the World Trade Center bombing and Kansi admitted to the murder of two CIA men outside the CIA headquarters. Both men relentlessly argued that their terrorism was aimed at punishing the US government for its policies towards Muslim countries. The stereotype prevailing in America is a caricature of men like Ramzi and Kansi. Moreover, films like *The Siege* are dwarfed opposite the current Muslim megastars known to America: Saddam Hussein, Osama Bin Laden, the Taliban, and the Unknown Terrorist. Admittedly, it is not easy being a Muslim in this country today, but this is a piece of the reality that American Muslims cannot control. What they can control is their own contribution to the reality: their response to it.

Whining about caricatures only shows an unwillingness to face reality. The cold-blooded calculus of self-interest that US foreign policy uses towards Muslim countries is certainly a cause for Muslim anger. But whether terrorism is an answer to the partiality of US foreign policy is a personal choice. American Muslims need to bravely make their minds up about terrorism by Muslims. If one believes in terrorism as an answer to injustice, one ought to be willing to take the heat for it—Osama Bin Laden does. If one is against it, it is easier to see that stereotypes that may cause random violence against American Muslims really emerge from the larger picture. Clarity brings a courage of conviction that quietly changes the stereotype.

There is a very clear and urgent alternative to whining for all American Muslims who see US foreign policy towards Muslim countries as unjust but who do not believe in terrorism. They should organize to present a strong, consistent, and reasoned criticism of US foreign policy while clearly condemning terrorism. The critical political objective has to be the separation of policy criticism from terrorism in the public mind. This is the role American Muslim groups should be seen playing. Trying to regulate what Hollywood and the television networks show can never be effective especially when your political voice has not quite cracked yet.

The Muslim community needs to separate Muslims from terrorists. It needs to forcefully clarify who is criticizing and who is resorting to terrorism. Whining can only change the stereotype of Muslims from a group associated with terrorism to a group of consistent whiners associated with terrorism.

Periodical Bibliography

The following articles have been selected to supplement the diverse views presented in this chapter. Addresses are provided for periodicals not indexed in the *Readers' Guide to Periodical Literature*, the *Alternative Press Index*, the *Social Sciences Index*, or the *Index to Legal Periodicals and Books*.

Sai'd Al-Ashmawy	"Islam's Real Agenda," *Reader's Digest*, January 1996.
Covert Action Quarterly	"Algeria: Theocracy by Terror?" Winter 1999.
William Dalrymple	"The Beast in the East," *World Press Review*, September 1996.
Koenraad Elst	"The Rushdie Rules," *Middle East Quarterly*, June 1998. Available from PO Box 3000, Denville, NJ 07834.
Steven Emerson	"Unholy War," *New Republic*, September 14–21, 1998.
Richard Grenier	"The Long History of Living in Terror," *Washington Times*, August 25, 1998.
Robert Kennedy	"Is One Person's Terrorist Another's Freedom Fighter? Western and Islamic Approaches to 'Just War' Compared," *Terrorism and Political Violence*, Spring 1999. Available from 900 Eastern Ave., Newbury Park, Ilford, Essex, IG2 7HH, UK.
Stefan Leader	"Osama bin Laden and the Terrorist Search for WMD," *Jane's Intelligence Review*, June 1, 1999. Available from Sentinel House, 163 Brighton Rd., Coulsdon, Surrey CRS 2NH, UK.
Bernard Lewis	"License to Kill: Usama bin Laden's Declaration of Jihad," *Foreign Affairs*, November/December 1998.
Najum Mushtaq	"Islam Distorted," *Bulletin of the Atomic Scientists*, July/August 1999.
Ahmar Mustikhan	"Different Faces of Islamic Fundamentalism," *World & I*, July 1999. Available from 3600 New York Ave. NE, Washington, DC 20002.
David D. Newsom	"Gauging War on Terrorism," *Christian Science Monitor*, August 26, 1998.
Frank Smyth	"Culture Clash—bin Laden, Khartoum, and the War Against the West," *Jane's Intelligence Review*, October 1, 1998.
Tim Weiner	"Missile Strikes Against bin Laden Won Him Esteem in Muslim Lands, U.S. Officials Say," *New York Times*, February 8, 1999.

CHAPTER 4

What Policies Should the United States Take Toward Islam?

Chapter Preface

In August of 1998, *Wag the Dog*, a Hollywood movie that depicts a president who declares war as a ruse to divert attention from his personal life, seemed to become a script for real life. In the midst of the scandal surrounding his relationship with Monica Lewinsky, President Bill Clinton fired missiles at six sites in the Muslim countries of Sudan and Afghanistan. According to Muslim-American writer Akbar Ahmed, Clinton's actions "confirmed, to the point of caricature, what many in traditional Muslim societies already believed—that America has little to offer the world but sex and violence."

Clinton and other policy officials, however, defended the air strikes as a necessary retaliation to the terrorist bombings of U.S. embassies in Kenya and Tanzania—believed to be the acts of Islamic fundamentalist Osama bin Laden. In an address to the nation explaining the attack, Clinton stated that "our target was terror. Our mission was clear—to strike at the network of radical groups affiliated with and funded by Osama bin Laden, perhaps the preeminent organizer and financier of international terrorism in the world today. . . . The risks from inaction to America and the world would be far greater than action."

Although most Americans agree that bin Laden poses a threat to the United States—as evidenced by his declaration that he intends to wage a war on the U.S., whom he calls the "Great Satan"—many argue that attacks against bin Laden and his allies will increase, not decrease, the risk of terrorism against the U.S. *New York Times* columnist Tim Weiner, explaining the views of counterterrorism officials, writes that "the [U.S.] missiles inflicted little lasting damage but helped to make Mr. bin Laden 'a revered figure' in the Islamic world"—thus bolstering his influence.

Because bin Laden has become an almost mythological figure for both the U.S. and the world of fundamentalist Islam, the question of how to deal with him influences many U.S. policy decisions toward Muslim countries. Other issues relating to U.S. policy toward the Islamic world are discussed in the following chapter.

> "We must on good intelligence engage in what the intelligence community calls 'anticipatory defense' [against Islamic fundamentalists]—or, in plain language, hit them before they hit us."

The United States Should Launch an Attack on Islam

Richard Grenier

In the following viewpoint, *Washington Times* columnist Richard Grenier warns that Islamic fundamentalists pose a serious threat to the safety of U.S. citizens. The only way to stave off this threat, Grenier argues, is for the United States government to launch a preemptive strike against fundamentalist nations. He argues that an attack of this kind is not overly aggressive, but rather a vital preventative measure against terrorism.

As you read, consider the following questions:
1. What delusion do Americans suffer from, in Grenier's opinion?
2. According to the author, how must America prepare for "the most morally difficult conflict in our history"?
3. What evidence does Grenier provide that the U.S. has been "lucking out" when it comes to Islamic terrorism?

Reprinted from Richard Grenier, "The Long History of Living in Terror," *The Washington Times*, August 25, 1998, by permission of *The Washington Times*. Copyright ©1998 News World Communications, Inc.

Now to all who think we've very recently entered a new age, the age of terrorism—where innocent civilians have suddenly become victims of terrorist attacks—I have a simple question: what are the civilians so afraid of in Lord Byron's following evocation of battle?

"And near, the beat of the alarming drum / Roused up the soldier ere the Morning Star; / While thronged the citizens with terror dumb, / Or whispering with white lips—'The foe! They come! They come!'"

My question is just what are the poor citizens (civilians) afraid of? The battle evoked took place during the Napoleonic wars almost 200 years ago. Both parties, dominantly French and British, were civilized, weren't they? Assuredly they wouldn't harm innocent civilians. But of this, judging by their "white lips," the citizens don't seem confident.

And what of the Cossacks, who during the Napoleonic wars laughingly burned thousands to death in the Russian retreat from Moscow? Or left thousands of other Russians without shelter to freeze to death in the coming winter? Or, if you'd like a change of scenery, how about the nearly three-quarters of the total German population that perished during the 30 Years War (while the Pilgrims were settling Massachusetts)?

For the fact of the matter is that until quite recently, despite Auschwitz, we've been living in a relatively brief hiatus in the history of war which, until perhaps a century or so back—and this since forever—was an uninterrupted tale of carnage, killing, destruction, rape, pillage, looting, murder, kidnapping, extortion, vandalism, incendiarism and gratuitous mayhem. This is the way the high-culture ancient Greeks fought wars, and (obviously) the Romans, Saracens, Crusaders and Nordic invaders. What happened to Carthage? When the Romans got through with it there was not a blade of grass left.

America's Delusion

In America we suffer from the widespread delusion that the relative peacefulness we've enjoyed for decades (and without even a missile defense system) should by rights last forever. But it won't. Some years ago Samuel Huntington of Harvard predicted that the coming great world conflict would be be-

tween the West and Islam. For no matter how kindly we behave—or no matter how well most of the Islamic population
behaves—we're separated by a gulf in material affluence that
is bound to incite extreme resentment. We, a technologically
advanced society, make at least some efforts to help those
less advanced. But those less advanced don't forgive us for
being rich.

Personally, I'd advise President Clinton, if he has the
moral stamina, to make not one anti-terrorist speech, but
dozens. The fact is that the American people have almost
completely lost their warlike spirit. And the danger is they
think the terrorist attacks at Khartoum and Dar es Salam are
flukes. [In August 1998, two U.S. embassies in Africa were
bombed, causing the death of over 200 people. The bombings are believed to be the work of Muslim terrorist Osama
bin Laden.] Osama bin Laden himself has promised they are
only the beginning. And I'm prepared to take his word that,
in plain fact, a war is now afoot between America and Islamic
fundamentalism. And also, still according to bin Laden
(along with Hezbollah, Hamas, etc.) that the Islamic Jihad
will fight this war for decades, and with no holds barred.

After all, as an Islamic fundamentalist once told me in Algeria, "When you bombed the Germans during World War
II, you never counted the innocent civilians you killed. What
Americans were worried about collateral damage then?"
One result of the protracted period of peace we've enjoyed
in America (augmented by remains of certain attitudes from
the Vietnam anti-war movement) is that we simply cannot
bear to kill civilians. Our adversaries of course don't mind in
the least killing civilians. In fact, as one told me on a recent
occasion, killing innocent women and children shows the
strength of their feelings. But God forbid American weapons
should produce "collateral damage." This is not the attitude
of a nation ready for war, and a war, furthermore, with no
visible end.

Preparing for an All-Out War

America is heading into the most morally difficult conflict in
our history, and to all appearances we need some toughening
up. A single resentful presidential speech the night after Is-

lamic fundamentalists bomb another American embassy isn't enough. Nor is a single day of mourning for the American dead. Before this thing is over, we're likely to lose quite a few more dead, and the country must be prepared for it. And we must prepare in ways we've usually reserved for all-out war.

President Clinton Explains His Decision to Launch an Attack on Afghanistan and Sudan

There have been, and will be, times when law enforcement and diplomatic tools are simply not enough, when our very national security is challenged, and when we must take extraordinary steps to protect the safety of our citizens. With compelling evidence that the [Osama] bin Laden network of terrorist groups was planning to mount further attacks against Americans and other freedom-loving people, I decided America must act.

And so, . . . based on the unanimous recommendation of my national security team, I ordered our Armed Forces to take action to counter an immediate threat from the bin Laden network. The United States carried out simultaneous strikes against terrorist facilities and infrastructure in Afghanistan. Our forces targeted one of the most active terrorist bases in the world. It contained key elements of the bin Laden network's infrastructure and has served as a training camp for literally thousands of terrorists from around the globe. We have reason to believe that a gathering of key terrorist leaders was to take place there . . . , thus underscoring the urgency of our actions.

Our forces also attacked a factory in Sudan associated with the bin Laden network. The factory was involved in the production of materials for chemical weapons.

The United States does not take this action lightly. Afghanistan and Sudan have been warned for years to stop harboring and supporting these terrorist groups. But countries that persistently host terrorists have no right to be safe havens.

William J. Clinton, Address to the Nation by the President, August 20, 1998.

Richard Haas, director for foreign affairs at the Brookings Institution, recently made some recommendations, some of which will surely curdle the blood of conventional liberals. We must make a much greater effort to obtain intelligence abroad. We must make more intensive our supervision of our own citizens (one can imagine how the ACLU [American Civil Liberties Union] will like this). And—here we tread on the most dangerous ground—we must on good intelligence engage in what the intelligence community calls "anticipatory defense"—or, in plain language, hit them before they hit us.

Before rushing to condemn such seemingly aggressive behavior we should recall that many members of our intelligence community consider that we've been lucking out for years. They're astonished that our enemies have so far used only conventional explosives in strikes on embassies, when their money gives them access to biological, chemical and nuclear weapons as well. Nuclear weapons or their ingredients produced by the late Soviet Union (or North Korea) are apparently going for bargain-basement prices.

A major preemptive strike against some rogue Taliban-controlled state—with dead women and children all about—would of course set off a terrific moral ruckus in America. But imagine the ruckus that would be set off if such a state set off a nuclear device in California. This is now the world we live in.

"*We have shown the world . . . that 'we take an uncompromising stand against terrorism'. . . by an act of terrorism.*"

The United States Should Not Launch an Attack on Islam

Arthur Hoppe

In the summer of 1998, two U.S. embassies in Africa were bombed—the suspected work of Osama bin Laden, a self-proclaimed Islamic fundamentalist who is implicated in numerous acts of terrorism. In response to the embassy bombings, the U.S. fired cruise missiles at the Muslim countries of Sudan and Afghanistan. Arthur Hoppe condemns the actions taken by the United States government in the following viewpoint, claiming that the U.S. attack was as much an example of terrorism as were the bombings in Africa. Hoppe is a columnist for the *San Francisco Chronicle*.

As you read, consider the following questions:
1. What is the definition of terrorism, as explained by Hoppe?
2. How have Osama bin Laden and President Bill Clinton justified their orders to bomb, according to the author?
3. How does the U.S. "demonize the enemy," in Hoppe's view?

Excerpted from Arthur Hoppe, "Terrorism vs. Terrorism," *The San Francisco Chronicle*, August 21, 1998, © The San Francisco Chronicle. Reprinted with permission.

"Oh, no," I said when I heard the news. "More terrorism."

Along with the rest of the country, I was appalled when Islamic fanatics blew up our embassies in Africa. But I was equally appalled when we bombed their bases. I see little to choose between these two acts of bloodshed.

Terrorism has been with us since the first caveman crushed his neighbor with his club. By definition, it is to "coerce by threat or force." It is the growling dog, the charging rhino; it is the law of the jungle.

The torturers in the dungeons of Torquemada believed in the effectiveness of terror. So does the mother who threatens to strike her recalcitrant child. The Japanese bombed Pearl Harbor to force us out of Asia. We bombed Dresden to force the Nazis to lay down their arms. Both are basically terrorist acts.

Terrorists naturally employ the most effective weapons in their arsenals. The Palestinians or the Islamic fanatics have no tanks, warplanes or intercontinental missiles to wage a conventional war against the military might of the Israelis or the United States. So they blow themselves up on the crowded streets of Tel Aviv or daringly drive their truck bombs through the gates of our embassies.

All terrorists, whether nations or individuals, must justify what they do. Osama bin Laden has said he and his men are fighting to drive the United States out of all Islamic countries. We, in turn, bombed suspected terrorist centers in the weak nations of Afghanistan and Sudan in order, said President Clinton, "to advance peace, democracy and basic human values."

We have shown the world, he said proudly, that "we take an uncompromising stand against terrorism." We have done so by an act of terrorism.

Our president quoted bin Laden as saying, "We do not differentiate between those dressed in military uniform and civilians. They are all targets." Mr. Clinton went on to excoriate the terrorist leader for condoning "the murder of innocent men, women and children."

I'm sure we hoped that our Cruise missiles, fired from hundreds of miles away, killed only Muslim terrorists in retaliation for their attacks. But I would be surprised if they killed fewer civilians than the 12 Americans who died in the embassy bombings.

As always, we demonize the enemy. To them, we are "The Great Satan." To us, those who drive truck bombs into embassy grounds are performing "a cowardly act." Yet our airmen who killed thousands of civilians in Dresden and Hiroshima were hailed as national heroes. We somehow distinguish between explosives delivered by a truck, a bomb or a Cruise missile.

Reprinted by permission of Chuck Asay and Creators Syndicate.

When I was young in World War II, I would have been an airman had I the chance. If I had been in a B-24 over Dresden, I would have gladly triggered the bomb release. I fear that all of us are terrorists in our hearts.

And this saddens me. I have long held that the human race has come a long, long way from the times of that first brutal caveman. But when I think of how capable we all are of acts of terrorism, I realize how very, very far we have to go.

"Muslims everywhere—including the millions now living in the West—are tired of the anti-Islamic tirades that pass for North American and European public discourse."

U.S. Policies Incite Islamic Terrorism

Haroon Siddiqui

In the viewpoint that follows, Haroon Siddiqui asserts that the United States plays a significant role in provoking terrorist attacks by Islamic groups. According to the author, U.S. foreign policies are often hostile or indifferent to Muslims. Siddiqui is the editorial page director and writer for the *Toronto Star*.

As you read, consider the following questions:
1. What is the "central fact" about the anti-American hatred that drives Islamic terrorists, according to Siddiqui?
2. How is America's foreign policy hostile or indifferent to Muslims, as explained by the author?
3. What "honorable exception" to America's usual foreign policy does Siddiqui mention?

Excerpted from Haroon Siddiqui, "Why Terrorists Target America," *The Toronto Star*, August 13, 1998. Reprinted with permission: The Toronto Star Syndicate.

145

[P]resident Bill] Clinton says [that] terrorist attacks are an inevitable result of America's global leadership role. "We act to advance peace and democracy."

Partly.

Several other factors contribute to the anti-American hatred that drives the terrorists. They are only the twisted and violent manifestation of a general discontent felt across the Muslim world against the United States, and the West generally. Not to grasp that central fact is to attack the symptoms, not the root causes, of the problem.

Anti-Islamic Tirades

First, Muslims everywhere—including the millions now living in the West—are tired of the anti-Islamic tirades that pass for North American and European public discourse.

Anti-Islamic prejudices come well-anchored in Western history—from the days of Christian Byzantium, the Crusades and the Inquisition. The surprise is that the demonization of Islam and Muslims, bordering at times on racism, persists, even among otherwise intelligent and sophisticated people.

Second, there is the geopolitical reality of America's foreign policy which is:

- Heavily pro-Israeli.
- Tolerant of gross human rights violations against Muslims—in Palestine, Bosnia, Kosovo, Kashmir, Chechnya. . . .
- Heavy-handed and selective in pursuing sanctions, against Iran, Sudan, Libya and Iraq.
- Indifferent to the plight of millions of starving and malnourished Iraqi civilians—despite several humanitarian appeals by UNESCO—and stubborn in pursuit of a morally bankrupt policy that has done little to weaken Saddam Hussein, let alone dislodge him.
- Allied with undemocratic and unrepresentative governments in many Muslim lands. Not unlike in Latin America in another era, America is in bed with many despots, dictators and monarchs, all oppressors in varying degrees—from Algeria to Kuwait, Saudi Arabia and Egypt. (In fact, it is the fear of an unknown alternative in Iraq

The West's Role in Islamic Fundamentalism

Muslim academics cite the reasons for the surge of Islamic fundamentalism in recent years as:

- U.S. support for Israel and a perceived lack of support for Arabs.
- Supposed Western abuse of military might in confronting Iraq during and after the Persian Gulf War.
- The West's harboring of those who poke fun at Islam (especially Salman Rushdie, author of *Satanic Verses*).
- Perceived Western double standards when it comes to democracy in Muslim countries such as Turkey and Algeria.
- Ditching of Islamic fundamentalists as soon as Western goals are achieved, as in the case of Afghanistan after the demise of communism.

Ahmar Mustikhan, *World & I*, July 1999.

that has led Washington into the swamp of loathing and tolerating Saddam at the same time).

A Perpetrator of Islamophobia

Of course, there are reasons and justifications for each of those policies. There are also several honorable exceptions—such as the humanitarian intervention in Somalia. But cumulatively, America is seen as no friend of Muslims, indeed as a perpetrator of much of modern Islamophobia.

This is not to excuse the intellectual failure of the Muslim world to come to grips with contemporary issues, on Islamic terms. The vacuum is filled periodically by revivalist movements, and, the odd time, by violent zealots.

But it equally ill-behooves America, and the rest of the West, including Canada, to remain blind to the sentiments and democratic aspirations of the world's 1.2 billion Muslims.

"The United States should strengthen its support of, and work more closely with, moderate Islamic governments making a serious effort to address the needs of their people."

The United States Should Support Moderate Muslim Governments

Edward P. Djerejian

In the subsequent viewpoint, Edward P. Djerejian contends that the United States should strengthen its support of moderate Muslim governments, promote the rise of free market economies within the Muslim world, and foster a dialogue among different religious groups. Although the United States should take a leadership role in the development of Muslim countries, he warns that the United States should resist imposing Western political models on traditional societies. Djerejian is the director of the James A. Baker III Institute for Public Policy at Rice University and former Assistant Secretary of State for Near Eastern Affairs.

As you read, consider the following questions:
1. For what reasons does Djerejian urge that the United States be sensitive to the complexities involved in the modernization process of the Muslim world?
2. According to the author, what role should the United States play in the Arab-Israeli conflict?
3. In Djerejian's view, what challenge does the United States face in regard to its policies on Islam?

Excerpted from Edward P. Djerejian, "The Arc of Crisis," *Harvard International Review*, Spring 1997. Reprinted with permission.

Some of the most important foreign policy challenges faced by the United States today involve Islamic movements. These challenges extend throughout an "arc of crisis" extending from the Balkans through the Caucasus, North Africa, the Middle East, and Central and South Asia. Though each of these situations has its own historic, ethnic, and political context, all involve Muslims asserting their identity and pursuing political goals against both non-Muslim and Muslim regimes. In Bosnia, Chechnya, Nagorno-Karabagh, Algeria, Gaza and the West Bank, Southern Lebanon, Afghanistan, and Kashmir, the rallying cry of Muslim fighters—"Allahu Akbar" ("God is Great")—is heard in a complex web of violent conflicts.

This is not a "clash of civilizations" but the manifestation of particular political, ethnic, religious, and cultural conflicts which have intensified in the post-Cold War era. Nevertheless, policymakers must now address religious and cultural factors which were not readily apparent during the bipolar confrontation between the United States and the Soviet Union. The realpolitik approach to foreign policy which prevailed during the Cold War was based largely on balance of power considerations and is insufficient to deal with the individual fires flaring along the arc of crisis .

The United States must recognize that the proliferation of local and regional conflicts in the arc of crisis threatens major, even vital, US interests. With three-quarters of the world's oil and gas reserves located in the arc of crisis , conflicts in this region have important consequences for energy supply, security, and pricing, especially for the United States and other industrialized democracies. . . .

Official U.S. Policy Toward Islam

Understanding these stakes is just the first step toward developing an effective policy. While I was Assistant Secretary of State for Near Eastern Affairs, the State Department elaborated a policy approach toward Islam which became the official position of both the Bush and Clinton Administrations. This policy holds that the United States does not consider Islam the next "ism" confronting the West, respects Islam as one of the world's great faiths, but objects to those who, whatever their religion, resort to violence, oppress minorities, preach intolerance, disdain political pluralism, or violate internationally accepted standards regarding human rights.

The United States also recognized that many Islamic movements are a response to social injustice, including the lack of economic, educational, and political opportunities in many countries. The United States therefore supports the expansion of political participation in these countries, but also is suspicious of those groups which might use the political process to come to power, only to destroy that process in order to retain political dominance. Responding to the cancellation of the 1992 elections in Algeria which the Islamists were poised to win, the United States emphasized that while it believes in "one person, one vote," it rejects those who would uphold only "one person, one vote, one time."

This overall approach is a valid basis for US policy, but the time has come to move beyond it in a more comprehensive way to face the challenges in the arc of crisis. To go beyond the present approach, the United States needs to frame a policy which acknowledges the broad scope of the challenge and is based on the following principles of action. First, the US government must make sure it has the organizational resources to better understand the depth and complexity of the forces at play in the arc of crisis as a whole, and thereby form the basis for realistic and effective policy planning and formulation. This should be a priority for the Central Intelligence Agency and the State Department's Bureau of Intelligence and Research. In addition, the State Department's Policy Planning Staff should be central to this overall effort, and the Foreign Service must develop the necessary regional expertise through area studies and language training, especially Persian and the Turkic languages of Central Asia. While establishing counter-terrorism policies and operations directed against financial and other support mechanisms for extremist groups is very important, this cannot be the major focus of policy. We must also not forget to include Indonesia (the world's most populous Muslim state where an important Islamic revivalist movement is underway) and Malaysia in our policy considerations.

Second, US policy must strongly differentiate in word

and deed between the Islamic mainstream and those Muslim individuals, groups, and regimes which work against US interests through violence, repression, and the quest for authoritarian rule. The United States should, as a consistent policy, encourage governments in the Muslim world to reach out to their societies on the dual track of broadening participatory government and free market forces as expeditiously as their particular circumstances permit. The United States should make clear its support for broadened political participation in the Muslim world with the key requirement for such support being the acceptance of the principle of the "alternance of power" according to the ballot box. The United States should strengthen its support of, and work more closely with, moderate Islamic governments making a serious effort to address the needs of their people for social justice, more participatory government, and economic growth through the free market. At the same time, the United States should promote privatization and market economies as the most effective approach to diminish the social injustice which gives rise to extremism. In so doing, however, the United States must be sensitive to the complexities involved: the modernization process of the West is viewed in parts of the world with suspicion and even hostility. Imposition of secular ideas can lead to resistance, particularly among those individuals and groups who are not sharing in the modernization process and who see themselves as its dispossessed victims. This is the breeding ground of extremism. That is why it is essential that the fruits of political participation, market reforms, and economic and social development are shared by the greatest number of people.

Engaging in Dialogue

A principal element of this approach is effective political dialogue between governments and a broad spectrum of their societies, coupled with viable economic policies that benefit large sectors of the populations involved and the creation of middle classes. The United States should tailor its approach to each country, with the understanding that we should not try to establish Western political models in many of these societies which are traditionalist in nature and have their own forms of political consultation, which can be expanded along the lines of Western democratic principles.

The United States does have close relations with key countries that can serve as positive forces for moderate Islam beyond their borders. These countries are coping with the dynamics of economic and social change and indigenous Islamist movements, including militant groups. The way these societies deal with these dynamics will influence, in no small measure, the future of the politics in the Muslim world. Turkey, with its secularist model of Muslim society and an Islamist prime minister in a coalition government with a secularist political party, is one example. . . .

Bridging the Gap Between Islamic and Western Values

We close this century with global markets and capital flows, emergence of new industries and the painful fading of others, the universality of service industries such as accounting and law, and the globalization of norms and values—[American] norms and values. . . .

The good news is that most people throughout the world, including those in non-Western countries, admire and imitate or import features of American political and economic organization. They want no part of [alleged terrorist] Osama Bin Laden or what he represents. Globalization will continue to spread the dominant American values of individual liberty and free enterprise. But there will continue to be a value gap between the United States and some non-Western societies. It must be bridged, or we must prepare for further episodes of blowback.

Charles Norchi, *Plain Dealer*, December 29, 1999.

Egypt and Saudi Arabia are other countries in which mainstream Islam and radical movements are contending, and where the way in which social and economic change occurs will influence the future of Islam and Islamism. In Egypt, home to Al Azhar, Islam's greatest university, an important debate is underway between moderate and radical Islamic thinkers. The Egyptian regime has been actively targeted by radical Islamic groups ever since President Anwar Sadat's assassination in 1981. Saudi Arabia, important for both its oil resources and its role as custodian of Islam's holiest places, is now contending with an indigenous Islamist movement which opposes the regime's domestic and foreign policies, and which has targeted the US military presence in the Kingdom and the Gulf. It is noteworthy that, at the conclusion of a conference of Arab Interior Ministers in Tunis in January, 1995, Saudi Minister of Interior Prince Naif Bin Abdul Azziz emphasized the necessity of collective Arab action to fight terrorism and the inaccuracy of the notion linking terrorism with Islam. Nevertheless, the United States must proceed realistically and without any grand illusions: each of these countries has to contend with internal problems involving Islamist political movements and groups.

The Arab-Israeli conflict has been a particularly important factor in forming Muslim attitudes toward the West, and the resolution of this conflict will help defuse anti-Western sentiment among Muslims and undercut the influence of the Islamist extremist groups, especially in the Levant. With the change in government in Israel and subsequent pause in negotiations with the Syrians and the Lebanese, and a focus on security issues and reciprocity with the Palestinians, it becomes even more important that US efforts to advance the Arab-Israeli peace process be accelerated. While much has been achieved since the Madrid Peace Conference in 1991, including the Oslo Accords and the peace treaty between Israel and Jordan, important opportunities have been missed and a comprehensive peace on all fronts has not been achieved. The United States has a critical role to play as the "honest broker" to assure that the principles of the Madrid peace process remain the basis of negotiations. The road toward a comprehensive peace will promote the urgently needed interests of both Arabs and Israelis for personal and state security, as well as economic and social development. If the process does not move forward in a timely manner, then the forces of extremism—both religious and secular—are more likely to prevail.

Building Bridges, Not Walls

Moreover, the US government must not only recognize the underestimated role of religion in international affairs, but it must also be prepared to complement political, economic and security policies with efforts aimed at fostering a dialogue among different religious groups.

Enhanced exchanges among Jews, Christians, and Muslims can only help promote peace and understanding in the Middle East. The establishment of diplomatic ties between the Vatican and Israel is an important step toward enhancing religious dialogue between Christianity and Judaism. The Organization of the Islamic Conference and the Muslim World League can expand their efforts to resolve inter-Arab disputes, for example, by reaching out as a point of contact with other religious groups and organizations to promote interfaith dialogue.

While religious differences have been and remain a cause or pretext for conflict, the work and actions of religious groups and individuals can help foster peaceful settlements. In the West, one could cite the many examples of people of religious faith acting politically when other approaches failed to resolve conflict: the Moral Re-Armament Movement following World War II and reconciliation between France and Germany; the role of the Mennonite Church in the conciliation talks between the Sandinista government and the Miskito Indians of eastern Nicaragua in the 1980s; the Catholic Church in the Philippines during the 1986 revolution; the Quakers and their role in the Nigerian civil war; the churches' work to help end apartheid in South Africa. . . .

The challenge before the United States on the eve of the new century is to determine how to maintain and develop its own set of values, and, at the same time, coexist and interact with other value systems and cultures which will continue on their own paths. The anthropologist Clifford Geertz contends that "you can't assert yourself in the world as if nobody else was there. Because this is not a clash of ideas. There are people attached to these ideas. If you want to live without violence, you have to realize that other people are as real as you are." By acting creatively and assertively in its relations with Islam and Muslim countries and movements, the United States can demonstrate real leadership at a critical historic crossroads.

Periodical Bibliography

The following articles have been selected to supplement the diverse views presented in this chapter. Addresses are provided for periodicals not indexed in the *Readers' Guide to Periodical Literature*, the *Alternative Press Index*, the *Social Sciences Index*, or the *Index to Legal Periodicals and Books*.

Akbar Ahmed	"Muslims, Missiles and Monica," *New Perspectives Quarterly*, Summer 1998.
Fouad Ajami	"The Region Left Behind," *U.S. News & World Report*, July 27, 1997.
Azizah Al-Hibri	"Legal Reform: Reviving Human Rights in the Muslim World," Harvard International Review, Summer 1998. Available from PO Box 3000, Denville, NJ 07834-9452.
Economist	"America and Islam: A Wobbly Hand of Friendship," August 26, 1995. Available from 111 West 57th St., New York, NY 10019.
Economist	"Living with Islam," July 27, 1996.
Conrad F. Goeringer	"God, Guns, Oil & Opium," *American Atheist*, Winter 1998–1999. Available from PO Box 140195, Austin, TX 78714-0195.
Shia Imami Ismaili	"Perspective from the Muslim World: The Right to Hope," *Vital Speeches of the Day*, September 1, 1996.
Arthur L. Lowrie	"The Campaign Against Islam and American Foreign Policy," *Middle East Quarterly*, September 1995. Available from PO Box 3000, Denville, NJ 07834.
Gary Sick	"A Look at . . . the Iranian Stalemate: They're Changing, Why Can't We?" *Washington Post*, March 28, 1999. Available from 1150 15th St. NW, Washington DC 20071.

Glossary

Allah God.

Allahu Akbar "Allah is Most Great."

ayatollah A high-ranking religious leader among *Shia* Muslims.

burqa The required garment for women in Afghanistan, which consists of a robe that conceals the head, face, and body, with a small piece of netting over the eyes.

chador The covering worn by women in Iran, consisting of a dark cloth that covers the head and body and conceals the figure.

Dar al-Harb Literally, "House of War"; the non-Muslim world that is deemed hostile to **Islam**.

Dar al-Islam Literally, "House of **Islam**"; the Islamic world.

Dawa Literally, "call"; signifies an invitation to join the faith of **Islam** or the spreading of the message of **Islam**.

faqih A legal expert in Islamic jurisprudence.

fatwa An interpretation of religious law issued by an authoritative scholar or leader.

fiqh Islamic jurisprudence.

hadith Traditions or sayings attributed to the prophet Muhammad in the writings of his contemporaries and referred to for authoritative precedent in interpreting the **Qur'an**.

hajj The pilgrimage to Mecca that is one of the pillars of the Islamic faith; all who are able are required to make the pilgrimage at least once in their lifetime.

hijab A veil that fully covers the hair, or, more broadly, the modest dress that is required of Muslim women by the *sharia*.

huddud Literally, "limits"; the limits of acceptable behavior; the specific punishments designated under *sharia* for specific crimes, such as intoxication, theft, adultery, and apostasy (disavowing the faith).

ijma Consensus of opinion among the community or the *ulama*.

ijtihad Independent judgment on religious matters or principles of Islamic jurisprudence that are not specifically outlined in the **Qur'an**.

imam Religious or political leader particularly among *Shia*.

Islam Submission to God and to God's message revealed to Muhammad; the religion of **Muslims**.

jihad Struggle; can be any struggle, from a personal striving to fulfill religious responsibilities to a holy war undertaken for the defense of **Islam**.

khalifah (often caliph) Literally, "successor" to Muhammad; the viceregent or political leader of the Muslim state.

mujahedeen (singular: *mujahed*) Persons who wage *jihad*.

mujtahid A person who exercises *ijtihad*.

Muslim A person who submits to God by following **Islam**.

niqab Garments worn by Muslim women that include a face covering and gloves.

pan-Arabism A movement seeking to unite the Arab nations of the Middle East and North Africa.

purdah A Persian word denoting the modest dress of women and the separation of women from men.

Qur'an (often Koran) Literally, "the recitation"; the text of Muhammad's revelations and prophecies; the Holy Book of the Islamic faith.

al-Sawa al-Islamia The "Islamic Awakening"; the term sometimes used to refer to the political **Islam** phenomenon.

sharia Literally, "the way"; the Islamic legal code as stipulated in the **Qur'an** and *hadith*.

Shia/Shi'ite Literally, "party" or "sect," specifically referring to the "party of Ali"; a **Muslim** who follows Ali (the cousin and fourth successor of Muhammad), who was deposed as leader of Muhammad's followers.

shura Consultation; the duty of a leader to seek the consultation of religious experts or the people.

Sunna/Sunni Literally, "path"; following the example of Muhammad set out in the **Qur'an** and *hadith*; refers to the majority Muslim denomination (as differentiated from *Shia*).

sura Chapter of the **Qur'an**.

Taliban (sometimes **Taleban**) An Iranian militia, which calls itself Islamic, that has imposed a strict fundamentalist regime upon the country of Afghanistan and denied the rights of Afghan women.

ulama (singular: *alim*) Religious scholars, leaders, and experts.

ummah Community; specifically the community of Muslims.

zina Illegal sexual intercourse, including fornication, adultery, rape, and prostitution.

For Further Discussion

Chapter 1

1. According to Srdja Trifkovic, what values does Islam promote? How does her view differ from that of John L. Esposito?

2. In what ways does Islam hinder the development of democracy, in Martin Kramer's view? How might the two reformers discussed in Robin Wright's viewpoint counter Kramer's claim?

3. Daniel Pipes claims that Islam suppresses freedom of speech. Ali A. Mazrui responds to this claim by pointing out that Western societies also practice censorship. Whose argument is more convincing, and why? In your opinion, is some measure of censorship necessary to the peaceful functioning of a society?

4. Based on your reading of this chapter, do you think conflicts between Islam and the West can be resolved? Why or why not? Provide a specific example to support your answer.

5. What assumptions does each of the authors in this chapter make about Islam? What assumptions do they make about the values of the West?

Chapter 2

1. What evidence does Ibn Warraq provide that the Qur'an believes women to be inferior to men? What evidence does Mahjabeen Islam-Husain provide that the Qur'an supports women's rights? Whose evidence is more convincing, and why?

2. According to the Revolutionary Association of the Women of Afghanistan (RAWA), in what ways does the Islamic Taliban oppress women? How does Hassan Hathout dispute the notion that the Taliban upholds Islamic beliefs? How would Mahjabeen Islam-Husain respond to RAWA's argument?

Chapter 3

1. On what basis does Robert W. Tracinski assert that Islam is a terrorist threat to the United States? How does Edward W. Said refute this claim?

2. Explain the contrasting definitions of *jihad* offered by Raphael Israeli and Mohammed Abdul Malek. What type of evidence does each employ to support their definitions? Whose evidence is more persuasive, and why?

3. Robert Fisk argues that media stereotypes of Muslims as terrorists lead to racism and discrimination against American Muslims. On the other hand, Kazim Saeed maintains that the

media depiction of Muslims does not define the image of Muslims. Which viewpoint do you find more convincing? Explain your answer.

Chapter 4

1. Richard Grenier suggests that the U.S. must defend itself from potential Islamic terrorism by launching a preemptive strike. Arthur Hoppe, on the other hand, argues that U.S. bombings of Muslim countries are an example of terrorism itself. Based on what you have read in these viewpoints, do you think that it is morally acceptable for the U.S. to attack its presumed enemies? Why or why not?

2. What assumptions does Richard Grenier make about Islam? How would Haroon Siddiqui respond to Grenier's assumptions? Support your answer with examples from the viewpoints.

Organizations to Contact

The editors have compiled the following list of organizations concerned with the issues debated in this book. The descriptions are derived from materials provided by the organizations. All have publications or information available for interested readers. The list was compiled on the date of publication of the present volume; names, addresses, and phone numbers may change. Be aware that many organizations take several weeks or longer to respond to inquiries, so allow as much time as possible.

American-Arab Anti-Discrimination Committee
4201 Connecticut Ave. NW, Suite 300, Washington, DC 20008
(202) 244-2990 • fax: (202) 244-3196
website: www.adc.org

This organization fights anti-Arab stereotyping in the media and works to protect Arab-Americans from discrimination and hate crimes. It publishes a bimonthly newsletter, *The Chronicle*; issue papers and special reports; community studies; legal, media, and educational guides; and action alerts.

American Muslim Council (AMC)
1212 New York Ave. NW, Suite 525, Washington, DC 20005
(202) 789-2262
website: www. amconline.org

This nonprofit organization was established to identify and oppose discrimination against Muslims and to raise the level of social and political awareness of Muslims in the United States. It publishes the biweekly *AMC Bulletin* and numerous pamphlets.

AMIDEAST
1730 M St. NW, Suite 1100, Washington, DC 20035-4505
(202) 776-9600 • fax: (202) 776-7000
website: www.amideast.org

AMIDEAST's educational programs and services are intended to promote understanding and cooperation between Americans and the people of the Middle East and North Africa. The organization publishes a number of books for all age groups, including *Islam: A Primer* and *The Rise of Islam*.

Anti-Defamation League (ADL)
823 United Nations Plaza, New York, NY 10017
(212) 885-7700 • fax: (212) 867-0779
website: www.adl.org

The Anti-Defamation League is a human relations organization dedicated to combating all forms of prejudice and bigotry. It publishes a wide range of materials on Israel, the Middle East, and the Arab-Israeli peace process, including *The Israel Accord* and *Towards Final Status: Pending Issues in Israeli-Palestinian Negotiations*. The ADL also maintains a bimonthly on-line newsletter, *Frontline*.

Arab World and Islamic Resources and School Services (AWAIR)

2137 Rose St., Berkeley, CA 94709
(510) 704-0517 • fax: (510) 704-0517
website: www.dnai.com/~gui/awairproductinfo.html

AWAIR provides materials about the Arab world and Islam for precollege-level educators. It publishes several books and videos about the Middle East and Islam and also hosts summer educational programs.

Canadian Islamic Congress (CIC)

420 Erb St. West, Suite 424, Waterloo, ON 2NL 6K6 Canada
(519) 746-1242 • fax: (519) 746-2929
website: www.cicnow.com

CIC's stated goals are to establish a national Canadian network of Muslim individuals and organizations; to act in matters affecting the status, rights and welfare of Canadian Muslims; to present the interests of Canadian Muslims to Canadian provincial and federal governments, political parties, media and other organizations; to investigate the cause of the anti-Islamic tone and attitude in the media and in political, educational, financial and business organizations; and to assist in the efforts of improving the social, economic, educational and spiritual conditions of Canadian Muslims, alleviating the suffering of Muslims throughout the world, and promoting peace and justice throughout the world. Its publications include the CIC newsletter, *Anti-Islam in the Media 1999*, and *Islam, Canada and Social Justice*.

Center for Middle Eastern Studies

University of Texas, Austin, TX 78712
(512) 471-3881 • fax: (512) 471-7834
website: http://menic.utexas.edu/menic/cmes

The center was established by the U.S. Department of Education to promote a better understanding of the Middle East. It provides research and instructional materials, and publishes three series of books on the Middle East: the Modern Middle East Series, the

Middle East Monograph Series, and the Modern Middle East Literatures in Translation Series.

Council on American-Islamic Relations (CAIR)
1050 17 St. NW, Suite 490, Washington, DC 20005
(202) 659-2247 • fax: (202) 659-2254
website: www.cair-net.org

CAIR is a nonprofit membership organization that presents an Islamic perspective on public policy issues and challenges the misrepresentation of Islam and Muslims. It fights discrimination against Muslims in America and lobbies political leaders on issues related to Islam. Its publications include the quarterly newsletter *CAIR News*, reports on Muslim civil rights issues, and periodic action alerts.

International Institute of Islamic Thought/Association of Muslim Social Scientists
1145 Herndon Pkwy., Suite 500, Herndon, VA 20170
(703) 471-1133 • fax: (703) 471-3922
website: www.iiit.org

This nonprofit academic research facility is concerned with the development of Islamic scholarship and thought. It publishes over three hundred books in both Arabic and English, as well as the quarterly *American Journal of Islamic Social Science*.

Islamic Circle of North America (ICNA)
166-26 89th Ave., Jamaica, NY 11432
(718) 658-1199 • fax: (718) 658-1255
website: http://icna.com

ICNA works to propagate Islam as a way of life within North America. It maintains a charitable relief organization and publishes numerous pamphlets in addition to the monthly magazine *The Message*.

Islamic Information Center of America (IICA)
Box 4052, Des Plaines, IL 60016
(847) 541-8141

IICA is a nonprofit organization that provides information about Islam to Muslims, the general public, and the media. It publishes and distributes a number of pamphlets and a monthly newsletter, *The Invitation*.

Middle East Policy Council
1730 M St. NW, Suite 512, Washington, DC 20036-4505
(202) 296-6767 • fax: (202) 296-5791
website: www.mepc.org

The Middle East Policy Council was founded in 1981 to expand public discussion and understanding of issues affecting U.S. policy in the Middle East. The council is a nonprofit educational organization that operates nationwide. It publishes the quarterly *Middle East Policy Journal* and offers workshops for secondary-level educators on how to teach students about the Arab world and Islam.

Middle East Research and Information Project (MERIP)

1500 Massachusetts Ave. NW, Washington, DC 20005
(202) 223-3677 • fax: (202) 223-3604
website: www.merip.org

MERIP is a nonprofit, nongovernmental organization with no links to any religious, educational, or political organizations in the U.S. or elsewhere. MERIP feels that understanding of the Middle East in the United States and Europe is limited and plagued by stereotypes and misconceptions. The project strives to end these limitations by addressing a broad range of social, political, and cultural issues and by soliciting writings and views from authors from the Middle East that are not often read in the West. Its newsletter, *Middle East Report*, is published four times a year, and MERIP offers an extensive list of other Middle East Internet resources.

Muslim Public Affairs Council (MPAC)

923 National Press Building, 529 14th St. NW, Washington, DC 20045
(202) 879-6726 • fax: (202) 879-6728
website: www.mpac.org

MPAC is a nonprofit public service agency that strives to disseminate accurate information about Muslims. Its goal is to achieve cooperation among various communities on the basis of shared values such as peace, justice, freedom, and dignity. The agency publishes information about issues of concern to the Muslim community, such as U.S. foreign relations and human rights policy.

United Association for Studies and Research

PO Box 1210, Annandale, VA 22003-1210
(703) 750-9011
website: www.uasr.org

This nonprofit organization examines the causes of conflict in the Middle East and North Africa, the political trends that shape this region's future, and the relationship of the region to other nations. It publishes a variety of reports analyzing U.S. policy on the Middle East and Islam, including *Islam and the West: A Dialog, The Agent—The Truth Behind the Anti-Muslim Campaign in America,*

The Politics of Islamic Resurgence: Through Western Eyes, Demonizing Islamic Revivalism, and *Political Islam: The Challenges of Change.*

Washington Institute for Near East Policy
1828 L St. NW, Suite 1050, Washington, DC 20036
(202) 452-0650 • fax: (202) 223-5364
website: www.washingtoninstitute.org

The institute is an independent organization that produces research and analysis on the Middle East and on U.S. policy in the region. It publishes numerous position papers and reports on Arab and Israeli politics and social developments. It also publishes position papers on Middle Eastern military issues and U.S. policy, including "The Future of Iraq" and "Building for Peace: An American Strategy for the Middle East."

Bibliography of Books

Mahnaz Afkhami, ed. *Faith and Freedom: Women's Human Rights in the Muslim World.* Syracuse, NY: Syracuse University Press, 1995.

Akbar S. Ahmed *Islam Today: A Short Introduction to the Muslim World.* New York: I.B. Tauris, 1999.

Lawrence Davidson *Islamic Fundamentalism.* Westport, CT: Greenwood Press, 1998.

Joyce M. Davis *Between Jihad and Salaam.* New York: St. Martin's Press, 1997.

Dale F. Eichelman and James Piscatori *Muslim Politics.* Princeton, NJ: Princeton University Press, 1996.

John L. Esposito and John O. Voll *Islam and Democracy.* New York: Oxford University Press, 1996.

Elizabeth Warnock Fernea *In Search of Islamic Feminism: One Woman's Global Journey.* New York: Doubleday, 1998.

Nilüfer Göle *The Forbidden Modern: Civilization and Veiling.* Ann Arbor: University of Michigan Press, 1996.

Yvonne Yazbek Haddad and John L. Esposito, eds. *Islam, Gender, and Social Change.* New York: Oxford University Press, 1998.

Fred Halliday *Islam and the Myth of Confrontation: Religion and Politics in the Middle East.* New York: I.B. Tauris, 1996.

Shireen T. Hunter *The Future of Islam and the West: Clash of Civilizations or Peaceful Coexistence?* Westport, CT: Praeger, 1998.

Samuel Huntington *The Clash of Civilizations and the Remaking of World Order.* New York : Simon & Schuster, 1996.

Martin Kramer *Arab Awakening and Islamic Revival.* New Brunswick, NJ: Transaction, 1996.

Rose Wilder Lane with Imad-ad-Dean Ahmad *Islam and the Discovery of Freedom.* Beltsville, MD: Amana, 1997.

William Maley, ed. *Fundamentalism Reborn? Afghanistan and the Taliban.* New York: New York University Press, 1998.

Judith Miller *God Has Ninety-Nine Names.* New York: Simon & Schuster, 1996.

Mahmood Monshipouri *Islamism, Secularism, and Human Rights in the Middle East.* Boulder, CO: L. Rienner, 1998.

V.S. Naipaul	*Beyond Belief: Islamic Excursions Among the Converted Peoples.* New York: Random House, 1998.
Salman Rushdie	*The Satanic Verses.* New York: Viking, 1989.
Edward Said	*Covering Islam: How the Media and Experts Determine How We See the Rest of the World.* New York: Vintage Books, 1997.
Jane I. Smith	*Islam in America.* New York: Columbia University Press, 1999.
Milton Viorst	*In the Shadow of the Prophet: The Struggle for the Soul of Islam.* New York: Anchor Books, 1998.
Mary Anne Weaver	*A Portrait of Egypt: A Journey Through the World of Militant Islam.* New York: Farrar, Straus & Giroux, 1999.

Index